Survival & Safety

How to survive emergencies, natural and man-made disasters – and just stay safe.

By Don Philpott

Copyright © 2015 by Don Philpott

All rights reserved. No part of this book may be reproduced in any form or by any electronic or mechanical means, including information storage and retrieval systems, without written permission from the author.

ISBN: 978-0-9728062-3-7

Printed in the United States by Whitehall Printing Company

Must Read Warning & Disclaimer.

This book lists many plants that have been eaten or used for medicinal purposes for centuries. However, this book is not intended to treat any medical conditions or health issues. The herbal uses listed are ones that have been documented in literature, both medical and non-medical, around the world. Readers must not try any of these herbal uses without first discussing them with their medical and health care providers. The author cannot be held in any way liable if the reader does not follow these instructions.

NEVER EVER put anything in your mouth if you do not know what it is.

REMEMBER you may be allergic to something others eat all the time.

ALWAYS seek permission first if you want to forage on private land.
It is **illegal** to forage on state park lands.

NEVER hunt critters without a permit or license if one is required and NEVER out of season – unless it is a true survival situation.

NEVER hunt critters that are protected. States often have different rules so check with that state's wildlife commission or similar body.

Contents

Introduction 6

Chapter One. Basic Techniques 8

Chapter Two. Shelter Construction 12
    Types of shelter 13

Chapter Three. Water 20
    Finding Water 20
    Producing drinkable water 23

Chapter Four. Fire 25
    How to build a campfire 25
    Fire Lighting 28

Chapter Five. Food 31
    Basic Nutrition 31
    Foraging tips 33
    Critters 40

Chapter Six. Weapons, Tools and Cordage 41
    Weapons 41
    Tools and Utensils 43
    Cordage 47

Chapter Seven. Field First Aid 49
    Basic treatments 50
    Medicinal Plants 55

Chapter Eight. Orientation &Navigation 57
    Orientation 57
    Weather Forecasting 59
    Signaling 61

Chapter Nine. Fishing & Trapping 63

Hunting	65
Fishing	69

Chapter Ten. Hiking and Survival Kits 70
    My backpacking/survival kit 74

Chapter Eleven. Natural Hazards 77

Chapter Twelve. Technological and Man-made Hazards 125
    Household Chemical Emergencies 131
    Nuclear Power Plants 135

Chapter Thirteen. National Security Emergencies 140
    Terrorism 140
    Bomb Threats 142
    Chemical and Biological Weapons 144

Chapter Fourteen. Everyday Survival 155
    Disaster Supply Kits 158
    Shelter 167
    Recovering from a Disaster 173

Chapter Fifteen. Travel Safe 180

The Author

Don Philpott has been writing and experiencing the great outdoors for more than 50 years. He has expeditioned, backpacked, climbed, canoed, ridden and skied throughout Europe, North America, Africa, Asia, the Arctic, Australia and New Zealand.

He cofounded *Footloose*, the first environmental outdoors magazine in the UK in the 1970's and has written more than 60 books on camping, campfire cooking, travel, personal safety and survival and the great outdoors. His latest book is *Edible Florida, a guide to many of the edible and traditional herbal plants of Florida and southeastern U.S.* It is available on Amazon.

He is an instructor with the University of Florida's Florida Master Naturalist program, a Certified Interpretive Guide and member of the National Association for Interpretation. As a member of the Wekiva Wilderness Trust and a volunteer at Wekiwa Springs State Park in Florida, he helps run the interpretive and educational programs and conducts Edible Florida and basic survival classes. He also serves on the Board of Friends of Florida State Parks Inc.

Much of this book is based on the six-hour Survival Boot Camps that have been held at Wekiwa and elsewhere and which, over the years, have attracted hundreds of participants. Each person has to bring two large black plastic garbage bags and a small knife. The garbage bag is the most useful and versatile survival item you can have with you. It can be carried in a pocket and has literally scores of uses.

Don specially developed the boot camp for family group participation so that everyone would know what to do if a hurricane, tornado or other natural disaster destroyed their home. Of course, all the techniques are good skills to use in the great outdoors. The boot camp covers survival basics, building a shelter, foraging for food and water and lighting a fire as well as field first – all the basic techniques you need to survive.

Introduction

Disasters can happen anytime, anywhere. A hurricane, tornado or wildfire could destroy your home. You could get lost while out on a stroll in the woods. Your vehicle could break down in a remote area miles from anywhere.

All of these could put you in survival mode and this would be made worse if someone with you was also seriously hurt.

Every year, millions of people around the world do lose their lives or have them seriously disrupted because of floods, tsunamis, wildfires, earthquakes, blizzards, hurricanes and so on. In today's troubled world, we face threats from terrorism, civil unrest, explosions and the possibility of chemical, biological or even nuclear attack. In a major disaster, rescue services will be overwhelmed so you have to be able to fend for yourself and that means knowing what to do in order to survive

You should know how to respond to severe weather or any disaster that could occur in your area – hurricanes, earthquakes, extreme cold or flooding. You should also be ready to be self-sufficient. This may mean providing for your own shelter, first aid, food, water and sanitation.

I have been on expeditions where there have been major equipment failures such as tents shredding in icy blizzards while overnighting on an Icelandic glacier. Knowing what to do – and being able to do it quickly in these circumstances is often the difference between life and death.

Being prepared and understanding what to do reduces fear and anxiety and greatly increases your chances of survival. Having the will and determination to survive is the most important tool in your survival kit.

Survival - Rule of Three

- Humans are highly unlikely to survive more than **3 seconds** if they panic.

  You wake up in the middle of the night and smell smoke. You jump out of bed and open the bedroom door – not realizing that there is a raging inferno outside which overwhelms you the second the door is open. Always stop and think before taking any action.

  Another good reason for staying as calm as possible is that the body uses calories up seven times faster during these adrenalin rushes.

- Humans cannot survive more than **3 minutes** without oxygen.

  The brain accounts for about 2% of a person's body weight but requires 20% of its oxygen and calories so as your brain is starved of oxygen you will start making irrational decisions

- Humans can't survive more than **3 hours** in extremes of temperature – hot or cold. You will die from hyperthermia (heat stroke) or hypothermia (cold).

- Humans can't survive more than **3 days** without water.

  You may live a little longer but your physical and mental state will be seriously impaired – more on this later.

- Humans can't survive more than **3 weeks** without food.

  After a while the body will start to eat its own organs, you will suffer anemia, then liver and kidney failure, blood toxicity, coma and death.

Chapter One. Basic Techniques

Before leaving – even on short trips – always let someone responsible know where you are going, the route to be taken and when you plan to get back.

Always carry as basic equipment: first aid kit, hat, map and compass, whistle, food and water (or know how to forage for them) and waterproofs. In hot climates, don't forget sun screen, insect repellent and lip balm. In cold climates have gloves. Even if you are only going for two-hour stroll in the woods pack your survival kit – you never know when you will need it.

In an emergency try to stay calm. STOP, THINK, OBSERVE and PLAN

STOP. Don't move unless it is dangerous to stay where you are. Is there a danger of falling rocks or flooding, are you too exposed? Assess your situation and the condition of yourself and colleagues – is anyone hurt? Stay calm and calm others in your group.
THINK. Do I know where I am, do I know a way out. Can I/we make it out? Is it better to stay where we are or to move on?
OBSERVE. Is it safe or hostile terrain? Is there an obvious path out? Are there materials we can use for shelter/fires if we stay? Is there nearby food and water?
PLAN. Process all available information before deciding. **Don't take any action until you have thought it through.** Whether you plan to stay put or move on develop a plan of action first.

Staying Put

If you decide to stay put you must first tend to any injuries and then build a shelter and fire, find food and water, gather more firewood and put out signals.
If it looks like you might be there for a few days keep busy with chores such as making tools, foraging and gathering wood, scouting the area, setting snares and traps and making your shelter as snug and comfortable as possible.
Remember your most important goal is to survive and the more comfortable you can make your surroundings the more your moral will be boosted.

Moving On
If you decide to move on you must ensure that you and your colleagues are able to do so and you must have a pretty good idea where you are going. Sometimes you will have no choice but to move – for instance, someone is seriously hurt and must get medical attention or you in the path of a wild fire.

Remember that for every one mile you stray from your planned route, you extend the search area by 100 sq. miles making it that much more difficult for rescue parties to find you.

If you do move on, mark your trail. Rip a t-shirt up into strips and tie one to a bush or branch every so often or bush mark your trail by bending a branch upwards at intervals so that the lighter underside is visible. This way if a search party finds your trail they will know which direction you are heading. Look for game trails heading in the direction you want to travel - the going will be easier and faster.

If lost in the hills it is usually best to follow a ridge - there is less vegetation and because of the height advantage, you may spot familiar landmarks. There are also likely to be few streams or wet areas.

If following a stream or river you may have to ford it. Remember vegetation is normally thickest closest to the water and there will likely be more insects.

Before attempting any crossing try to determine the depth of the water. Walk up and down stream to see if there is a quieter stretch of water with easier access in and out. When crossing a wide river take a course across the current at about a 45 degree angle downstream

Traveling on snow and glaciers needs extra caution because you can never be sure how solid the ground is or what lies beneath. All members of a party should be roped together when crossing glaciers. If you need to climb up a snow-covered slope it is best to kick steps into the snow as you make your way diagonally up. To descend, slide down on your feet astride a strong stick that can be used as a brake. Never walk close to the edge of a cliff or steep slope. Always be aware of the danger of avalanches.

The Three elements of survival are:

- **Shelter (which includes clothing and fire).** Use all available materials to stay warm and dry.
- **Water – the most important** – for every 1% of body weight lost from sweating, you lose 10% of your efficiency and cognitive functioning. A 10% loss of body fluids will cause dizziness, confusion and severe headaches; a 15% loss leads to loss of vision, inability to walk and then, in most cases, death.

Remember - you can always find water in the wilderness.

- **Food.** You need water and food to function efficiently. And this is even more important in a survival situation.

Why you need to keep dry

You lose 20 times more heat when your clothes are wet than when dry. It is better to take your clothes off, put them in a garbage bag and sit on it until it stops raining. Your skin is waterproof. Then you can put dry clothes back on again. Also, the warmer and drier you are the better able you are to sleep –and sleep is vital for survival.

Clothing tips

Pants are generally better than shorts – they provide more protection from insects, undergrowth, sunburn etc.

Wear loose fitting comfortable, quick drying pants/slacks with belt loops.

Wear long sleeved shirts – sleeves can always be rolled up.

Wear sensible footwear. Sandals are OK around the campsite but you need more support on rugged trails.

Layering is the way to go. Add lightweight layers to stay warm and remove them to cool down.

Tip: a quick way to cool down is to wet your wrists with cold water.

Chapter Two. Shelter Construction

Some survival manuals suggest that if the weather if fine you can delay building a shelter but I would caution against that. If the weather is fine it is the best time to build a shelter and certainly preferable than scurrying around once it starts to rain or night falls.

Choose your site carefully – do you have enough suitable materials to build a shelter or natural features that you can use. If not, look elsewhere. Can things fall on you – dead wood overhead or loose rocks on nearby slopes, will the site flood, and are you too exposed to the elements? Check the surrounding area for scat and other signs of large animal usage.

My experience is that it is best not to construct your shelter in the open where it may be seen from above. I prefer as much protection as possible although close to an open space where you can set out signals and fires to attract rescuers.

Shelter criteria - protection from elements – level surface, heat retention, ventilation, drying facility, safe from natural hazards and stable (you don't want it falling down with the first gust of wind).

Tips: Shelters facing southeast tend to get morning sun and afternoon shade. Shelters near rivers even when high enough to be safe from flooding, can be damp in the mornings and if you are in a steep valley you will not get the early morning sun.

Types of shelter

There are many types of shelters and the one you pick depends on how many are in the group, how long you expect to use it and the likely weather conditions to be faced.

One person shelters - Bivvy bag/garbage bags

For years I have slept out under the stars in a Gore-Tex bivvy (bivouac) bag that is seven feet long and weighs six ounces – imagine a sleeping bag without the filling. It is wind and waterproof with a hood large enough for me to sit up and still be protected. My pack acts as my pillow or back support if I am sitting upright.

In a survival situation, black garbage bags come into their own. If it is a warm dry night, put one on the ground as an insulating layer and use the other as a sleeping bag. If it is cold, put one bag inside the other and fill the space between with leaves thus converting it from a one season bag to an all-season sleeping bag.

Squirrels nest – For a quick survival shelter scrape out a small hollow and gather a huge pile of leaves and burrow in among them. Downside to this is that as you move about you will lose most of your leaf cover.

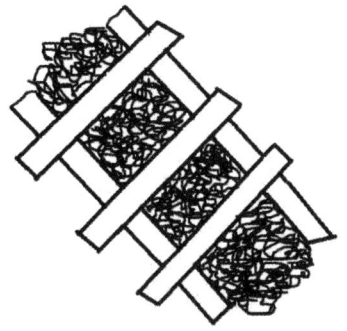

To minimize this, place two fallen logs side by side so that you have enough room to lie down on your back between them. Fill the space between the logs with leaves and compress them as you pack them in. If the logs are tall enough you can stack other logs across to help prevent dislodging the leaves.

If you prefer to sleep under cover:

Debris hut – wedge a pole in a low fork of tree or lash to the stump of a tree. Add uprights as below and then fill all gaps with leaves and other suitable materials. The inside of the hut should also be stuffed tight with leaves and soft vegetation.

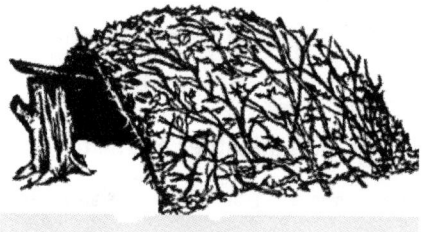

Emergency blanket/garbage bag poncho tent

Tie some string between two trees and use an emergency blanket or a couple of garbage bags to make an improvised tent.

Lean-To's and A-Frames

Lean-to and A-frames are larger with more storage space and room to move around a little but they can also lack insulation so in cold weather usually require a fire outside with a reflector shield to reflect heat into the structure.

With practice it is possible to build a very adequate lean-to or A-frame shelter in about an hour especially if you have two or three people working together as a team. Some of the structures built in our Survival Boot Camps have been incredible. Build the shelter before it gets dark so that you can get inside and see any light coming through gaps in the thatching. That gives you time to add more leaves and material as weather proofing. Gather bedding material and test it out. If it is uncomfortable gather more. You want to be as comfortable as possible so that you sleep well and wake up ready to take on whatever the new day has to throw at you.

Lean-To

Wherever possible use existing trees for additional support and strength. Your ridge pole is your anchor with uprights lashed to it. Cross poles provide additional strength and a base for thatching (see below). Once thatched, cover the roof with thick layers of leaves and other material for added insulation and waterproofing. If you are inside the shelter and can see any light coming in – you will get wet if it starts to rain.

A-Frames

An A-frame is really two lean-to's side by side. They can be free standing although it is always best to utilize natural solid supports such as trees. Lash uprights and cross poles together for additional stability.

Thatching.

Traditional thatching involves bundles of grasses or reeds that are laid side by side and tied to the crosspieces of the shelter. Start at the bottom, complete the row and then move up. Each row overlaps the one below by several inches to create a waterproof finish. This is the method used on English cottages for centuries where a thatched roof can last for 300 years.

If you don't have access to grasses or reeds, use branches of leaves, banana leaves or palmetto fronds. Again start at the bottom and work along and then up. This sort of roofing does not produce a thick thatch so once finished it is important to get into the structure and see where all the gaps are – and then get out and fill them. One way to add extra waterproofing and insulation is to pack dry leaves into the leaves and then cover the roof with an additional layer of leaves. When finished, you should be able to go inside your shelter and not see any daylight.

In my survival kit I always carry two large black garbage bags and if I need to construct an A-frame these can be used over the ridge pole for additional waterproofing.

If you are building a lean-to, A-frame or debris hut it is also a good idea to construct a 'door' – a structure that can be used to close the entrance or in the case of a lean-to, to seal off one of the open sides if that is where the wind is blowing from.

Underfloor heating. Scoop out holes four to six inches deep in the sleeping area, add hot stones from fire and cover with a thick layer of soil. If the rocks are too near the surface you risk burning yourself while you sleep.

Cordage

Your survival kit should contain parachute cord or similar but it takes a lot of cordage to lash everything down in a shelter. Luckily nature does provide a lot of materials that can also be used. In Chapter Six we discuss making cordage from several materials and all of this can be used when constructing your shelter. Young vines and flexible stems of many plants can also be used.

Other shelters

Desert Shade shelter – to protect you from the sun but not waterproof. Good for desert and mountain desert survival. Incorporate something that already provides shade – a rock or tree – and then gather material to lean up against it so that you have room to shelter beneath. Ideally you need enough material to prevent sunlight getting inside the shelter. If there is not enough material to do this use clothing to plug any gaps.

Tip: When gathering materials use caution. All sorts of critters might be sheltering beneath it from the sun. Use a stick to prod the pile and to turn pieces over.

Sapling hut – in areas with lots of close growing saplings pull several together and tie the tops together to form a hoop shelter. Then weave branches in between to create your shelter.

Ground shelter – excavate a hole big enough for you to lie down in and cover with large plastic bag/emergency blanket weighted down by rocks or pieces of wood. Obviously only use this shelter in areas that will not flood.

Use natural features – hollow and fallen trees, slopes, caves, rocks, depressions in ground can all be used for survival shelters. Clear ground of rocks and debris and stuff the inside of the shelter with as much insulation as possible (grass, leaves and so on). You need to be able to burrow into this vegetation layer rather than lie on top of it. Have a backup supply right outside the shelter so you can top up inside as you compress the first layer. Once inside you can also pull this pile of leaves into the structure's opening to help seal it.

Snow shelters

Snow cave

Some years ago I was among a group of four outdoors writers asked to test a new range of high mountain clothing. We were 'invited' to spend a night sleeping out on the Bionnassay glacier which is around 8,000 feet on Mont Blanc – without sleeping bags or tents.

The heavily insulated jacket and pants proved remarkably effective for almost four hours but we then agreed that it was prudent to take shelter. We quickly excavated a snow cave where we spent the rest of the night very comfortably.

Snow holes are easy to dig out by 'gloved' hands if the snow is firm. Inside you need to fashion a ledge to sit on and store gear, a lower ledge to rest your feet on and below that a sump to hold the melting snow. Even if it is many degrees below freezing outside, the temperature inside will quickly rise to well above freezing, especially if you have three or four people sharing it. An added advantage is that the melting snow collecting in the sump is also your source of drinking water. It is important to have ventilation so stick a ski pole or ice axe through the roof to allow fresh air in and stale air out. If it is snowing and the airshaft is getting blocked jiggle the ski pole to re-open it. Do not use a stove in a snow hole as carbon monoxide will build up.

Snow hole

If the depth of snow or lie of the land does not allow you to build a snow cave look for a large tree with snow piled up around it and burrow into it for a shelter.

Unless you are an expert don't think about building an igloo even if the snow conditions are right. It takes a lot of skill and effort and your first few attempts are likely to collapse. The other snow shelters mentioned above are easier and quicker to construct using less calories.

Chapter Three. Water

You can't survive for long without water and that is especially true if you are trekking through an arid wilderness. Water constituents about 60 percent of total body weight and every system and organ in your body depends on it. Even when you are sitting in an armchair watching television, you are losing water through your breath, perspiration and then more when you go to the toilet. The average sedentary adult male loses up to 1.3 liters of water this way every day.

Put on a heavy pack and start hiking over difficult terrain and you really start to sweat. A walker carrying a heavy pack in these conditions can lose up to a liter an hour from perspiration. In very hot conditions you can lose up to 3.5 liters. Sweat a lot in cold weather and you can get hypothermia, sweat a lot in hot weather you can develop heatstroke, both of which can lead to death.

That is why you must drink lots of water and other liquids to replenish lost fluids, minerals and electrolytes. And, in order to drink a lot of water you have to have access to it.

Drinking water when eating is beneficial because it aids digestion but if you are running low on water, avoid eating fatty foods because they require more body water to break them down.

Finding Water

If you are stranded in the wilderness, you must be able to locate water, collect it and clean it before you can drink it. The easiest way to do this is to look at a map not just so that you know where you are, but to enable you to locate streams, lakes and other geographical features where water might collect.

Before setting out to find water, however, make sure you have something to collect it in. A collapsible plastic bucket or plastic bottle is fine for larger quantities. A heavy duty plastic bag works fine and a spoon or straw will allow you to scoop up tiny quantities.

Mountains

You are more likely to find water at the foot of a gentle slope than a steep slope. Follow valleys down looking for springs, pools or streams. If the vegetation suddenly gets very lush, look for water nearby.

Countryside

You shouldn't have trouble finding water in the countryside although you will have to purify it. There are a few things worth remembering. A row of alder or willows in the distance usually indicates a stream. A line of grass much taller than the rest could indicate a water source. During the spring, many trees, including maple and birch, contain water with a high sugar content. In an emergency, gouge a hole in the trunk (use a knife or stone) and then use a piece of bark to funnel the escaping liquid into a container. Cottonwood, sycamore and elder only grow where there is plentiful water. In the early morning, mop up dew and squeeze into your mouth or a container. Gather it before dawn because it will evaporate quickly as the sun rises. Check out low lying areas, muddy areas

Animals know where to get water, so follow tracks. Bees only live in areas where there is water. If you see wild bees you know that there is water within a mile or two. Note which direction they seem to be flying and use that to plot a path.

In tundra areas there are lots of streams and don't be put off by the brown, peat-stained water. You can drink it but strain it first and then purify it.

Desert

If you see birds or green vegetation or both together, there is usually water nearby. Be cautious, however, because the water may also attract wild animals. Many desert plants, especially cacti, contain water. Dew often forms on rocks around dawn and you can lick this to get some moisture. You may also find traces of water dripping from the roofs of caves or running down large cracks in a rock.

Good places to look for water are dry stream beds. Dig down and you may find damp earth, dig further and you may find water. Don't waste energy though. If the hole looks unproductive, try elsewhere. Other likely sites are at the foot of cliffs or rock outcrops, depressions or holes in rocks. Use a cloth to filter sand out of the water

Tropics

Water is not usually a problem. There are frequent downpours and areas of standing water. Many trees, plants and vines contain water like the banana. Chop the banana plant down to leave a stem about three feet (one meter) above the ground. Scoop out the center of the stem and it will start to fill up with water from the roots. It will continue to provide water for two or three days so cover the stem to protect the water from insects and birds. However, be on the lookout for bees because, as stated above, they only live near water.

Glaciers and snow-laden areas

There is no problem getting water in areas where there is ice and snow. The problem is that it takes energy to convert either into drinkable water. Melt ice rather than snow because it will yield more water. If you have to melt snow, melt a little at a time and then add more.

Purifying water

As a general rule, purify all water from rivers and lakes. There are places where the water is still pure and can be drunk from a mountain tarn or fast running stream but it is always better to be safe than sorry. There are bacteria and other contaminants in many streams, springs, and water sources, so filter or boil all drinking water if you are away on a long trip. The last thing you want is an upset stomach or worse from drinking polluted water. Depending where you are, untreated water could give you dysentery, cholera, typhoid and all sorts of parasitic infections.

Boil, purify with tablets or use a filter to produce drinkable water. Boil water for at least three minutes to purify it. An alternative is to add three drops of iodine to about 1 liter and let it stand at least 30 minutes before drinking.

You can use large filters to purify water in big containers and you can buy filter straws that can be used to suck up water from small pools. Once the filter is full, no more water can be sucked. This means that you can safely use it to get clean water from even the foulest looking liquids.

If scooping up larger amounts of water, let it stand for between 30 minutes and an hour to allow silt and sand to settle in the bottom of the container and then filter. Don't disturb the silt.

Always carry water with you but know how to find more if that runs out. In Good water sources in southeastern U.S. are:

Palms, especially date palms – cut low branches close to trunk and water will trickle out

Coco Plum – fruits contain lots of water

Prickly pear cactus – both fruit and lobes contain water

Sword fern – roots have white pea-shaped water reservoirs

Florida betony (rattlesnake weed) – white carrot-like roots bursting with water

Saw palmetto – leaf axles contain water and insects (protein)

Grape vines – cut vine close to ground and then make a notch about six feet from the ground. Place cut end in container and water will flow from the base.

All succulent plants

Air plants (bromeliads)

Producing drinkable water

Solar still

Dig a hole and place container in the bottom. Suspend a plastic sheet over the hole held down by stones at the side and pushed down in the center to form a dip over the container. Adding a few small stones will maintain the dip. Make a small hole in the plastic to allow water to drip into the container.

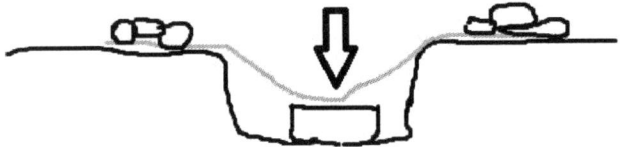

Dew trap – similar to above but no hole needed. Water gathers in the dip.
Rain trap – you can either use a plastic bag/sheet to trap the water or set up a series of collection points. Gather large leaves and twist them to form funnels with large open ends. These can then be suspended over containers to catch the rain.
Vegetation still – Fix a large plastic bag around bunches of leaves at the end of a branch and use twine and a stake to hold the branch down at a 45 degree angle. The leaves will continue to breath and give off water vapor which is collected in the bag. Obviously choose non-poisonous trees or bushes.
Ground solar still – similar to above but you can use low lying shrubs on slopes. Attach the plastic bag around the end of the branch so that it rests on the ground exposed to sunlight. The more sunlight it gets the more water will be produced.
Ankle rags – wrap a spare pair of socks or other pieces of clothing around your ankles and walk through dew-laden grass. Then wring out the socks for the water.
Plastic bag – in extreme situations place a plastic bag loosely over your head and breathe out. The water vapor in your breath will attach to the inside of the bag and you can lick it.
Filtration – use commercial filtration straws or filtering devices. In an emergency, use socks or other articles of clothing as filters.

Chapter Four. Fire

Fire offers security, warmth, the ability to cook and purify water and drive off animals. Smoky fires will repel insects and attract rescuers. Fire building and lighting is a skill and one that should be practiced so that you are totally proficient long before you hit the trails.

How to build a campfire

Basic techniques: To light almost any fire you need tinder, kindling and fuel. Tinder must be easily ignited from the spark or flame so that it flares up lighting the kindling which generates the flames and heat needed to ignite the fuel.

Tinder is usually dry grass and leaves, small twigs, wood shavings, sawdust, dead pine needles or the shredded dry inner layer of bark. It really should be dry although birch bark burns even when wet. You can even gather the lint in the linings of your pockets!

Tip: Carry a plastic Rx container stuffed with wood shavings, cotton wool and lint for emergency kindling.

For kindling, gather dry twigs, old bird nests, and strips of fallen bark, pine twigs or improvise with pieces of paper or strips torn from the bottom of your shirt.

Tip: Insect repellents often contain inflammable substances. Test yours at home on a piece of paper and see if it flares up. If it does, you can always use the repellent to help light a fire in difficult conditions.

Use larger dead branches, dried scat and dry grass twisted into bunches for fuel. Add your fuel one log at a time otherwise there may not be enough oxygen to sustain combustion and make sure you have an adequate supply of wood before you light your fire. Split softwoods, especially pine and fir, burn well because of the resin, and are good to get the blaze going but then switch to hardwoods which burn slower with less smoke and they provide better embers for cooking.

Tip: To tell hardwood from softwood, strip the bark away and run your finger nail along the wood. You will leave a mark in softwood but not in hardwood.

Build your fire slowly. All fires need oxygen and the biggest mistake most people make is to pile a lot of wood on once there are some flames. Rather than get a nice blaze you will smother the flames.

Tip: When gathering firewood, always collect two to three times more than you think you will need.

Choose a site protected from strong winds so that the fire does not blow out, burn too quickly or spread. A lightweight emergency blanket can be used to create a windbreak, build one from fallen timber or stack up rocks or soil. Clear the area around the fire to minimize the danger of it spreading.

If you are cooking on the fire, locate it some distance from your shelter to avoid accidents and in case the smell attracts wild animals.

If you are winter camping, make sure snow on overhead branches is not going to crash down and put the fire out. Always try to build a fire on a firm, flat base. You can use stones in an emergency to make a base as these will stay hot for many hours. Be careful in selecting stones and rocks, however, as wet or porous rocks may explode when hot. You can use wet dead logs to contain the fire and the heat may dry them out enough so they can be used later as fuel.

In woods or scrubland always clear the surrounding area to prevent the fire spreading. Scrape vegetation away to reveal the soil below which is safest and you should always try to restore the area before you leave.

Tip: Eat cold white ashes from the fire if you are constipated, eat black ashes to stops diarrhea!

Tip: One way to start an emergency fire taught by the US Air Force is first find a suitable place to light the fire and then gather enough kindling and fuel to keep it going overnight. Select two sturdy dead logs about two feet in length and with a diameter of four to six inches. Place them on the ground so that they form a right angle pointing into the wind. Place your tinder in the crook of the angle so that the logs act as a windbreak. Once ignited, slowly add kindling so that it is leaning against the two logs so that it catches fire but does not smother the tinder. As the fire becomes more intense, add your bigger fuel logs.

Continue this process until you have a roaring blaze. Slow and steady is the motto when it comes to lighting a fire. Make sure the tinder is well ablaze before adding a little kindling. Don't add too much tinder at any one time because you may smother the fire by starving it of oxygen.

Fire Building

Build a fire ring (stones, large logs etc.) and a reflector (using logs etc.) to maximize heat

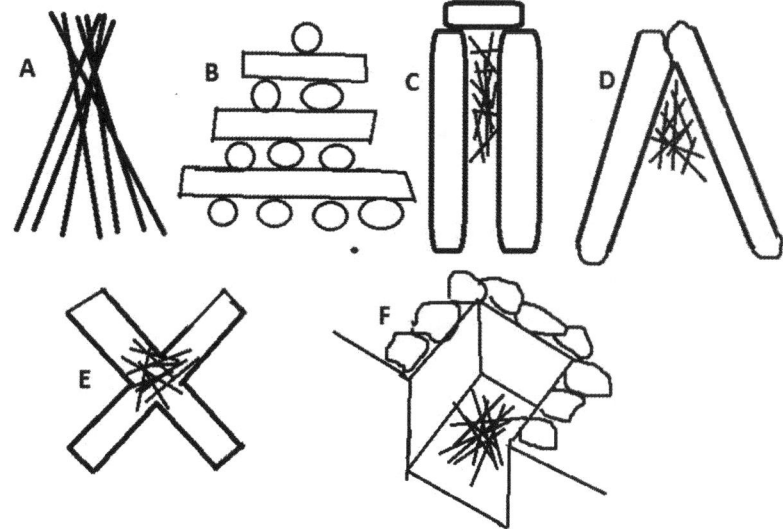

A. Teepee fire – easiest to build but needs frequent refueling

B. Pyramid fire – good all night fire needing little maintenance as fire is concentrated in the center of the pile and upper logs fall in providing the fuel source.

C. Long fire – good fire for cooking. Easy to maintain, can't get out of control. Pots can be stood on the two large logs. Embers can be moved away from the main fire to provide area to keep food warm.

D. Trapper's fire. Same idea as the long fire except that the fire is contained in the apex formed by the 'V'.

E. Star/Cross fire. The most versatile cooking fire. Dig a cross about four to six inches deep. The fire is built in the center and embers can be moved into different arms of the cross for keeping items warms, slow cooking and so on. You can also heat large stones in one arm of the cross and use as a griddle.

F. Pit fire – good cooking fire in exposed conditions. Dig a pit about one foot square and one foot deep. Build your fire in the bottom of the pit where it is protected from the wind and elements. You can hang pots from a branch spanning the top of the pit.

Some other cooking methods

Fire Lighting

There are many ways of lighting a fire if you don't have a box of matches available and it is a good idea to learn some of these techniques. However, matches or using the back of a knife blade on a magnesium fire steel to produce sparks are still the best and easiest options.

Bow and drill – very efficient but complicated to construct until you get the hang of it.

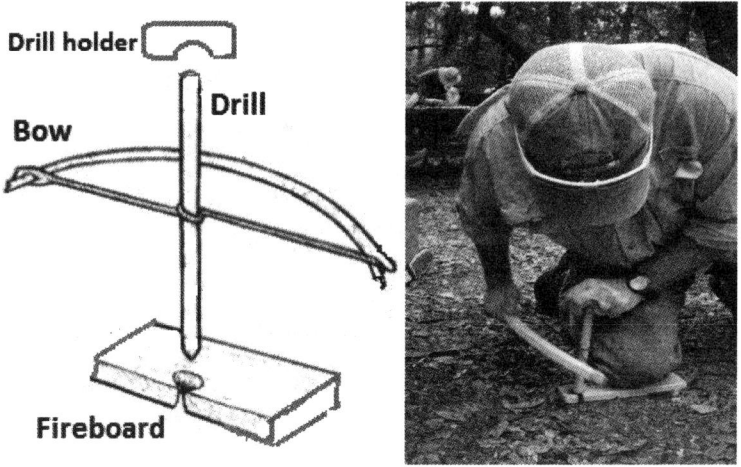

I like the bow to be strong and about the length between my elbow and tips of my fingers and it must have a little flexibility. I use parachute cord for the bow string. I like the drill to be hard wood (about eight inches long and about half an inch in diameter) and the fireboard to be softwood. Some people use hardwood for the fireboard but I think more friction is created by hardwood on softwood. The drill tip fits into a round hole carved into the fireboard from which there is a narrow channel leading to the edge of the board. Place a leaf with a pile of tinder up against the entrance to the channel. The top of the drill is held in place by another piece of wood, shell or similar.

The drill, held in place by the bow string, rotates when the bow is moved rapidly back and forth. The friction creates heat in the hole in the fireboard and minute pieces of hot wood from the sides of the hole pass through the channel and ignite the tinder. You can then carefully – and quickly - lift the leaf containing the tinder and use it to ignite the kindling.

Hand drill – is a simplified version of above – rub a softwood stick between your hands into a notch in a baseboard surrounded by tinder.

Fire plough - softwood base 12-16 inches long and 4 inches wide with a groove cut lengthwise. Kneel down so that the base rests diagonally from your thigh to the ground. Use **a** stick to plough up and down the groove. The friction causes small pieces of heated wood to be dislodged and ignite.

Mirrors and almost any other shiny reflecting object can also be used to start a fire if the sun is out. You can also use magnifying glasses or a knife blade.

Chapter Five. Food

Basic Nutrition

The U.S. Sierra Club calculated that you need two and a half times as many calories to gain 1,000 feet of elevation as you do to walk at sea level for one hour at 2 mph. For example, an adult needs between 350 and 500 calories an hour to cover 2 miles over rough but relatively flat terrain. To cover the same distance in the same time but ascending to 3,000 feet that same adult would need between 850 and 1,250 calories.

Even if you are out walking for just a few hours during the winter months, you will need more energy just to keep the body warm. In very hot weather, your energy requirements may be fewer but your liquid requirements increase. Sweating from exertion can lead to dehydration and hypothermia in cold weather, and dehydration and heatstroke in the summer. In winter, the problem is compounded by having to wear several layers of clothing. It has been estimated that a walker carrying a 35-pound pack in difficult terrain in very hot weather can lose up to 1 liter an hour from perspiration in addition to normal daily water loss of about 1.5 liters through breathing, sweating and urinating. If you sweat a lot it is important to change into dry clothes when you get the chance and whether you sweat a lot or not, it is vital to drink lots of liquids.

Anyone walking in the wilderness in the cold has to increase calorie intake both for energy and to keep warm. If you happen to be backpacking in the hills and carrying a heavy load, your calorie intake could soar to 4-5,000 calories a day or more for an adult male.

Food planning – knowing what to take with you and why - is critical when heading out into the great outdoors.

The three basic ingredients of your diet are protein, carbohydrate and fat. In the city if you are leading a sedentary job and eat a normal diet, you want to reduce fat intake because it is easily metabolized into body fat. In the wilderness, you need fat in your diet because if you are walking you are burning lots of calories and you need to convert fat into energy to fuel the body. Peanut butter is a great fat for the outdoors.

Simple carbohydrates – found in candy and fruit - provide a quick rush of sugar which can be an instant energy boost but it isn't sustained and can leave you feeling even more fatigued. That is why complex carbohydrates, like vegetables, nuts, seeds and grain, are better The body takes longer to break down complex carbohydrates so they are released more slowly into the system and their effect is longer lasting.

Protein – meat, fish, cheese and so on – are essential for general wellbeing. They also help build muscles and repair damaged tissue.

So, for maximum energy on the trail consume fat together with complex carbohydrates and protein. You want food that not only provides energy but that is healthy and above all, tastes good

For every day you are away, work out exactly what you will be eating for breakfast, lunch and dinner having chosen meals that provide the right energy and nutrition balance for the trip you are going on.

Then ensure you have enough to feed the entire party. In addition, make up snack packs (nuts, energy bars, comfort bars and so on) so that each person has one labeled pack for each day they are away.

It may sound unnecessary but it does make life so much easier on the trail if everything is labeled. Gather together a day's rations and pack and label breakfast, lunch and dinner ingredients separately and then put them together in their own container marked with the day the food is to be eaten. Repeat this so that you have each day's rations self-contained in their own pack. Always remove food from its commercial packing and place in sealable bags to reduce bulk and garbage.

Then you simply divide the food up between the members of the party so that the weight is reasonably distributed throughout the group. Each member carries his or her own supply of snacks and also has one or more complete daily meal rations - just in case they get separated from the group.

Dehydrated foods have the advantage that they are light, easy and quick to prepare. Manufactured dehydrated meals are nutritionally balanced and readily available. They are also easy to cook. Simply add water, bring to the boil, simmer for a few minutes and eat. Other one-person meals simply require you to add boiling water to the food packet. You stir, leave for five minutes and then eat. We always pack some dehydrated meals because apart from providing 'fast' food when you are really tired, they also make excellent emergency rations.

You can dry fruits, vegetables, mushrooms and meats to reduce bulk and give them an extended shelf life. Take them with you for healthy snacks or to add to soups, stews and other recipes. You can even prepare entire meals and dehydrate them. They can then be frozen or stored in airtight bags until needed. When you leave for the trail they will take up less room in your backpack and be a lot lighter to carry.

Foraging tips

Foraging for food can be fun if you want to add some interesting and nutritious ingredients to your meals or need a handy trail-side snack. It is different from foraging in an emergency when your ability to find food could save the lives of you and your family. However, knowing what to forage for is a skill that will enhance your appreciation of and enjoyment in the countryside and is something you can do as a family.

You can supplement your food supplies if you know the right things to pick from nature's abundant free larder. If you are camping you can add exciting new ingredients to your cooking and if you are under the weather, nature has a remedy to combat most ills.

Leaves, roots, flowers, berries, nuts and fruits can be picked but plants should not be destroyed in the process. Exercise special care when harvesting roots to ensure the plant will survive. A living plant can be a constant supply of food year after year.

The rule is, of course, don't pick anything unless you are absolutely sure of what it is and know that it is safe. If in doubt, leave it alone. A plant that is safe for one person might cause an allergic reaction in another –simply touching the leaves could be enough to trigger it. If you are eating a plant for the first time that you know is edible, caution is still necessary. Try a little bit first to see if you are allergic to it. If not, tuck in. In this way you can build up a list of the plants that you know you can eat safely. Remember that even though a plant is edible, too much of it might be a bad thing. Many wild plants, such as wood sorrel, contain oxalic acid which is harmful if consumed in large quantities, but oxalic acid can be found in similar concentrations in many everyday kitchen plants such as rhubarb and spinach. The moral is 'eat everything in moderation'.

Some basic foraging rules

Never ever put anything in your mouth unless you are absolutely certain what it is.

Just because some parts of a plant are edible, others might not be. Know what parts can be eaten raw and what needs to be cooked. Some plants are toxic when raw but safe when cooked.

Don't eat if it looks old, smells bad, has milky or discolored sap.

Choose picking sites carefully.

If it smells like almonds but isn't an almond it probably contains naturally occurring cyanide so don't eat it.

However, if it smells like onions, garlic and mint even though it is none of those, it is usually edible.

Most wild plants are bitter when eaten raw. Cooking reduces the bitterness.

Many wild plants contain oxalic acid which can cause a tingling in the mouth and in high quantities, a burning sensation which may lead to kidney damage. Baking, drying or roasting will often remove the oxalates.

Plants can have many edible parts some of which may not be available at the time you are foraging. However, keep a diary of these plants and their locations so that you can return later to forage from them.

If harvesting bark, strip it from branches rather than the tree trunk.

All grass seeds are eligible and when ripe make great trail-side snacks.

In an emergency use the touch "edibility" test (see below).

Remember: All plants are edible once!

Always know what you are eating. Many plants look similar, some are safe while others are not. Even the same plant can have some parts that are safe to eat and others that are inedible or poisonous and even the same part of the plant might be safe to eat or not depending on the time of the year.

People can react to eating plants in different ways. One person can eat a particular plant with no side effects while another may experience a range of reactions from nausea and diarrhea to cramps and headaches. For instance, if you are very sensitive to poison ivy it is advisable to avoid other plants in the same family i.e. sumac, mango and cashews.

Universal Edibility Test (UET)

There are many plants throughout the world. Tasting or swallowing even a small portion of some can cause severe discomfort, extreme internal disorders, and even death. This test was developed by the UK's Special Air Services (SAS) and is now used by most militaries around the world. If you are in a survival situation and have no idea whether or not the plants around you are edible, use this test to find out.

Only test a plant if it is abundant. There is no point in going through the whole process if there are only two or three plants available. Remember test each part of the plant separately according to the UET.

Even after successfully testing a plant, eat it in moderation until you know what effect it has on you. For instance, eating a lot of wild apples, especially on an empty stomach, is going to give you stomach cramps or worse.

1. Test only one part of a potential food plant at a time.

2	Separate the plants into its basic components—leaves, stems, roots, buds, and flowers.
3	Smell the food for strong or acidic odors. Remember, smell alone does not indicate a plant is edible or inedible.
4	Do not eat for 8 hours before starting the test.
5	During the 8 hours you abstain from eating, test for contact poisoning by placing a piece of the plant part you are testing on the inside of your elbow or wrist. Usually 15 minutes is enough time to allow for a reaction
6	During the test period, take nothing by mouth except purified water and the plant part you are testing.
7	Select a small portion of a single part and prepare it the way you plan to eat it.
8	Before placing the prepared plant part in your mouth, touch a small portion (a pinch) to the outer surface of your lip to test for burning or itching.
9	If after 3 minutes there is no reaction on your lip, place the plant part on your tongue, holding it there for 15 minutes.
10	If there is no reaction, thoroughly chew a pinch and hold it in your mouth for 15 minutes. Do not swallow.
11	If no burning, itching, numbing stinging, or other irritation occurs during the 15 minutes, swallow the food.
12	Wait 8 hours. If any ill effects occur during this period, induce vomiting and drink a lot of water.
13	If no ill effects occur, eat 0.25 cup of the same plant part prepared the same way. Wait another 8 hours. If no ill effects occur, the plant part as prepared is safe for eating.

CAUTION

Test all parts of the plant for edibility, as some plants have both edible and inedible parts. Do not assume that a part that proved edible when cooked is also edible when raw. Test the part raw to ensure edibility before eating raw. The same part or plant may produce varying reactions in different individuals

The following plants are all common to North America. To learn more about the flora that grows in your region or the area you plan to visit, buy a good edible plant identification guide and go out with a local edibles expert. The skills you learn will serve you well and could save your life.

Some of the plants that can be eaten raw on the trail or added to salads
Beauty berry, Biden's Alba, Bitter cress, Blue porter weed, Burdock, Chickasaw plum, Chickweed, Chinese elm, Creeping Charlie, Chicory, Cucumber weed, Dandelion, Day flower, Dock, Dollar weed, Eelgrass, False hawk's beard, Florida elm, Glasswort, Hercules club, Mustard, Nettle, Ox-eye daisy, Pilewort, Pink sorrel, Penny weed, Pennywort, Peppergrass, Persimmon, Plantain, Purslane, Red maple leaves, Saw palmetto, Saxifrage, Shepherd's purse, Smilax, Sorrels, Sow thistle stem, Spiderwort, Tansy, Trilliums, Violets, Watercress, Water hyssop, White clover, Wild garlic, Wild lettuce, Wild mint, Wild sorrel, Yucca and many, many more.

Roots, pollen and other parts that can be dried/roasted and crushed for flour
Buckbean, Bulrush, Cabbage palm, Cattails, Clover, Crowfoot seeds, Greenbriers, Hazel nuts, Kudzu, Pickerelweed, Prickly pear, Purslane, Sunflower seeds, Tamarack, Walnuts, winged yam, Acorns from white oaks, and inner pine bark can all be ground for flour.

Greens

Amaranth, Burdock, Chicory, Chickweed, Clover, Comfrey, Dandelion, Dayflower, Field pennycress, Fireweed, Greenbriers, Lamb's quarters, Mallow, Marsh marigold, Nettle, Pepper grass, Pilewort, Plantain, Pokeweed, Sea Purslane, Shepherd's purse, Sorrel, Sow Thistle, Spiderwort, Thistles, Trilliums, Violet, Wild lettuce, Wild mustard. Winter cress, and Wood nettle.

Roots and tubers that can be eaten as potatoes/vegetables – boil or roast

American lotus, Arrowroot, Bulrush, Burdock, Cattails, Chicory, Dandelion, Groundnuts, Jerusalem artichoke, Solomon's seals, Spurge nettle, Water chestnut, Wild onion, and Yellow pond lilies.

There are also nuts, berries and other fruits to enjoy, as well as a host of plants that can be used as herbs and seasonings – common tansy, ground juniper, horseradish, peppergrass, red bay, sea lettuce, wild garlic, wild ginger, wild leek, wild mustard and wild onions.

Plant Preparation

Many plants can be eaten raw – as trail snacks or in salads – while others must be cooked either to make them edible or more palatable. Plants that are edible provide nutrients but may taste horrible. Plants that are palatable are enjoyable to eat, like wood strawberries. Unfortunately, very many plants fall into the edible and not the palatable category. However, there are ways to improve flavor and edibility.

One of the greatest leaps early humans made was when they started to cook their food. Cooked food is easier to digest and generally more palatable. That means you use less calories to digest the food than if it was raw. In a survival situation that is very important. It is better to cook your food and have a hot, easily digestible meal so that the calories you save can be better used on staying alive.

Soaking and boiling leaves, stems and buds can reduce bitterness and tenderize the plant. It can also reduce saltiness. Sometimes you have to boil twice, throwing away the water from the first boil. Tubers and roots can be roasted, boiled or baked and often taste better for it. Drying is a good way to remove oxalic acid, found in many plants, especially members of the Arum family.

Leaching is a centuries-old technique to remove bitterness especially in acorns. Crushed acorns are placed in a strainer and boiling water poured over them. Alternatively, the sieve can be immersed in cold running water. Lots of plants can be eaten raw but many of them are better cooked. Grains and seeds can be eaten raw until they ripen when they become dry and hard. Then grind or boil them and use as flour. Young leaves and shoots can be eaten raw and added to salads. They are often rich in proteins, vitamins and minerals and low in calories. Older leaves tend to have more fiber and will have lost some of their goodness.

Use plants like red bay, wild garlic, wild mint and sea lettuce as natural flavorings to spice up other dishes and the sap from trees such as maples, birches, walnuts and sycamores as natural sweeteners. Very young leaves from the maple also make a natural sweetener.

If you have a glut of plants or berries, you can juice, freeze, sun-dry, pickle or dehydrate them.

Critters

If it moves, crawls, swims or flies – eat it.

All black beetles are edible raw but grubs, grasshoppers, termites and other insects are best cooked – add them to the stewpot.

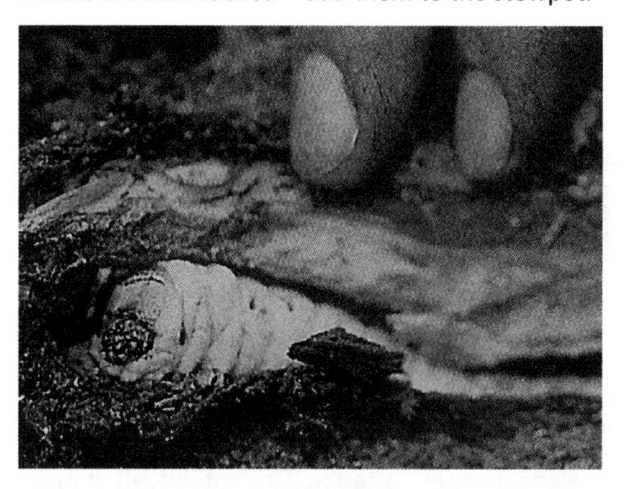

Witchetty grubs found in Australia's outback (see above) are a high protein food – eat raw or pan fry - yummy!

Chapter Six. Weapons, Tools and Cordage

A good knife is your best survival tool but it is amazing what you can improvise with once you start looking around. Shells, bones, pieces of wood and stones can all be used as tools, weapons or utensils. The tips of saw palmettos can be used as needles or fish hooks.

Weapons

Spears and throwing spears

Spears need to be four to eight feet long. You can either sharpen a point at one end, lash on a knife for a more efficient spearhead or improvise using a piece of rock or bone. If sharpening the spear harden the point in the fire. Spears can be thrown or used to stab at large prey.

Fishing spear. A straight sapling six to eight feet long is good. Cut off the top to get a flat surface and then use a knife to cut a cross into the top. Tie cordage tightly around the sapling about 9 to 12 inches below the top. Then using the knife blade and a piece of wood, split the sapling down to the cordage. Repeat creating another split at right angles to it. This gives you a shaft with four prongs which can be sharpened. Small pieces of wood can be inserted into the splits to keep them open. (See Chapter Nine for fishing techniques).

The Atlatl, or spear thrower, is a millenniums-old device that enables spears to be thrown further, faster and with more force. Experts are also able to throw it with remarkable accuracy. The atlatl allow you to hunt animals that are difficult to get close to as well as attack large animals because of the extra force (killing power) generated by the atlatl.

A basic atlatl is simply a long narrow strip of hard wood (two to three feet long) with a notch at one end in which the end of a four to six foot spear (dart) rests. The thrower grips the atlatl at the farthest point from the notch with finger tips holding the spear in place. The atlatl becomes an extension of the arm. The spear is launched in an action similar to serving a tennis ball. As your arm swings through the air the atlatl acts as a lever becoming upright in your hand before propelling the spear towards its target.

You can improve accuracy and the power of delivery by adding finger loops for a better grip.

Rabbit sticks are simply pieces of wood – 16-20 inches long - that can be thrown at rabbits and other small game. Use your knife to make the stick as smooth as possible so that it makes the least amount of noise flying through the air. Also, the smoother it is the more accurate it will be when thrown. It must have enough weight to be able to stun or kill the prey but not so heavy that it cannot be thrown easily. As with the atlatl it is a good idea to practice with the rabbit stick and become proficient at throwing it. Put a tin can on the ground, back away and then see if you can hit it. Practice makes perfect and the better you are the greater your chances of having rabbit stew.

Knives

I always carry a small knife on my belt. When I am hiking or backpacking, I carry two on my belt with a third in my backpack. The small knife is a Spiderco with 2.5 inch serrated blade that will cut though almost anything and can be opened with one hand. I also carry a Smith and Wesson CK114L dagger folding knife with a 4.9 inch blade. This knife opens with a flip of the wrist and the dagger-shaped blade means it can be lashed to a pole to make a fishing or hunting spear. The knife in my pack is forged from a single piece of steel with an eight inch long blade. It is virtually indestructible and can be used as a weapon and digging tool or a hammer if using end of the haft.

I think that you should be able to open all knives with one hand. If you are holding something in one hand that needs to be cut you must be able to open your knife with the other. Also, remember the guy that got his hand irremovably stuck while out hiking. He had two choices. He could stay stuck and starve to death or be attacked by wild animals or he could amputate his arm and get out of there. He chose the latter and survived to tell the tale. That is why two knives on your belt are a good idea. The dagger to cut through the flesh and the super-sharp serrated one to go through the bone.

Tools and Utensils

Stones can be used as tools in many ways. They can be used as hammers when setting snares and traps. If you have caught an animal, you can use a stone to crack the bones to get the highly nutritious marrow and if you have great skill you can make stone knives, axes and arrow heads.

Stone knapping is the art of striking one piece of stone (the hammer stone) against another so that flakes are carefully removed to create a cutting edge that can be used as a blade or a scraper to clean fish or a hide. Experts can craft very sharp, effective tools but the end result for most people is just bloodied and bruised fingers. Stone pecking is a lot easier and certainly more practical for most people. It involves hitting a soft rock with a hard rock. The impact causes the softer rock to shatter. Small flakes might be suitable for gutting fish while larger ones could be used as arrow or spear heads.

Wood can also be used for tools and utensils. Pieces of wood can be used as hammers or clubs. Small pieces can be fashioned with a knife into spoons. Large pieces can be fashioned as bowls or cooking pots. You gouge out the center with a knife or burn it out using hot wood from the fire.

Containers
Make containers from bark that you can cook with or use as mess cans. Birch, cedar and pine all have relatively smooth bark that you can work with but experiment with other trees as well. Birch is very pliable so one of the easiest to work with. Choose a reasonable thick limb from which to harvest your bark. Cut all the way round the limb. Make your second parallel cut about one foot away and then make a final straight cut between the two. Use the tip of the knife to carefully raise the bark along this last straight cut and then slowly work your fingers underneath gently prizing the back away from the tree. The aim is to remove a single large intact piece of bark.

Stretch the bark out on a firm surface with the outside of the bark facing down. You may have to wet the bark a little to make it more workable. Using the back end of a knife blade make score marks similar to those below making sure you do not go all the way through.

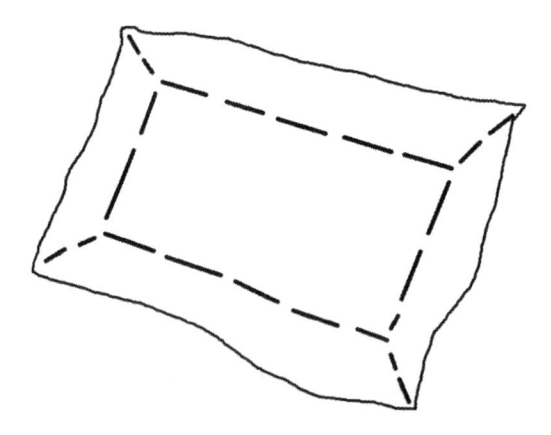

You then carefully fold all the sides up with the overlap at each corner being on the outside. Sew each corner together having carefully made holes for the stitches without tearing the bark and don't make the stitches too tight to avoid tearing. Alternatively you can make wooden pegs to hold each corner in place. Take a four inch twig about half an inch in diameter and make a three inch slit down the center. Slide the slit carefully over the bark so that all the corner pieces are held securely. The container should last several days as long as you are not cooking directly on the fire but use it suspended over it.

You can use bark for other types of containers. You can shape it into a funnel and pinch one end and use it to carry water or for gathering berries.

Clay Pots

If you have access to clay you can make primitive pots. You can often find clay in river and lake beds or in the ground. If you dig clay from the ground it will be dry. Crush it using a rock until it is fine particles and then slowly add water to rehydrate it. After a few hours the clay will be ready for molding.

If collecting clay from a river or lake you will have to separate it in a large water-filled container from other materials and debris. Leave it for a day and the contents of the container will have separated with rocks and sand on the bottom, clay above that and with a layer of organic material on top which can be skimmed off. Empty out a small amount of water and allows the contents to settle again and repeat this process until the layer of clay is exposed. Remove the clay being careful not to disturb the layer underneath and dry on a rock in the sun for several hours.

Add a little water and work the clay in your hands into a round snake-like length and then bend into a circle. If it does not crack it is good to work with. You can temper the clay by adding a little sand and then thoroughly combining it.

The easiest way to make the pot is to make several snake-like lengths and then coil them to form a round base and then to build up from that. Keep the clay and your hands moist – but not too wet - and use your fingers to smooth the clay so that all the coils merge. You can also smooth out any cracks you see. When you have finished let your pot dry in the shade so that it dries completely.

To fire the pot stand it near a wood fire to allow it to warm up and then after about 30 minutes place it on top of the ashes in the fire. Cover with sticks which will cover the pot with ash as they burn and then add more sticks to increase the heat for about two hours. After that let the fire down but do not remove the pot. It is important that it cools very slowly to prevent cracking. When it is completely cool it can be removed from the ashes and put into service.

Pine needle baskets

You can make baskets by weaving pine needles into coils and securing with stitches using raffia or other suitable materials and a blunt tapestry needle. In Florida we use long leaf pine needles as they are the longest – anywhere up to 15 inches in length.

Gather the needles and soak them in boiling water for 10-15 minutes and then remove and dry. Long leaf pine needles come in clusters of three joined together by the fascicle (sometimes called the head or cap). If you are making an elaborate basket you can remove the heads for aesthetic reasons but I leave them on.

Start with the base. Thread the raffia through the tapestry needle and then take five or six clusters of needles and hold them together. Start wrapping the raffia around them. As you wrap the needles start to curl them round until you have two circles. Push the needle through the center and start stitching the circles together. You should still have some protruding needles and these are used to extend the base.

You will constantly have to add new pine needles and raffia as the basket progresses. To add more pine needles take a cluster of five or six and push them into those protruding. As you continue to make coils with the old and recently added pine needles keep adding raffia stitches to hold everything in place. Be consistent when adding new pine needles so that the basket has some uniformity. You add more raffia by tying one end of the new piece to the exposed end of the old piece.

The size of the base will determine the size of your basket. For a medium size basket complete 6 to 8 circles and then start to weave the sides. Begin the sides by placing the next coil on top of the outside circle of the base and continuing round the outer edge, securing with raffia as you go. Repeat this process until you have the desired height. Stitch the pine needles securely in place and then cut off any surplus for a tidy finish.

Digging stick

Digging sticks have been used for centuries by tribesmen around the world and remain the Australian aborigines most use useful took. They should be about two foot long and between one and two inches in diameter. One end has a sharp point and the other end has a flat chisel-like blade. Hardwood lasts longer than softwood. The sharp point is good for breaking up the earth and the flat blade is good for digging.

Thousands of years ago they were adapted as primitive plows to create the furrows in which seeds could be planted. Now they can be used for digging for roots or getting to burrowing animals or termite larvae. You can also use them around the campsite for digging latrines and so on.

Cordage

You can make cordage from all sorts of naturally fibrous materials and when braided together it can be amazingly strong. Strips of rawhide (if you have had a successful hunt) as well as dried sinews and tendons can be used for lashing. Yucca (Spanish bayonet) is one of the best plant materials but you can also use bark, grasses, other large leaves, young, flexible vines and pliant stems.

Yucca can be used by simply stripping the leaves into long strips about a quarter of an inch wide. Longer, wider leaves grow on the outside of the plant and are the best ones to gather but remove the sharp tips before working with them. These strips are very strong and can be used as is for ties but it is better to braid two or three together if you want to use the braiding for lashing a shelter together. If you have the time you can produce incredibly strong cordage by extracting the fiber from the pulpy leaves and then braiding them.

Place the leaf on a large flat stone and then using the back edge of a knife run it down the leaf pressing the pulp out of the way. This has to be repeated several times before the fibers are exposed and can be gathered.

Braiding technique.

1. Bend a length of fiber so that it is double thickness with a loop at one end and two loose ends at the other.
2. If right handed, hold the loop securely with the thumb and index finger of your left hand.
3. Using the thumb and index finger of your right hand take the top strand and twist it away from you and then bring it towards you and fold it over the untwisted strand. It is important to ensure the twist is not lost because this prevents the cord from unravelling.

4. Take the untwisted strand and twist it away from you and then lay it over the other strand next to the first fold. Continue by alternating twists away and folds toward you. As you braid move your left hand down the cord to keep everything firm.
5. To splice in new strands, double over another strip of fiber and insert the loop so that it is up against the last fold. For a while you will be braiding two strands at a time but by the time you run out of the original strand the new splice will be securely in position.
6. Continue until you get to the desired length of cordage.

Braiding is not difficult but it takes practice to become really good at it. You can braid together as many strands as you want depending on how strong you want your cordage to be. There are lots of 'how to' braiding videos on youtube.com

Chapter Seven. Field First Aid

Everyone should go on a first aid course/CPR and if you spend a lot of time in the back country, take a field first aid course as well. While it is good to know what to do in the event of a medical emergency, your actions will often be dictated more by where you are rather than the injury itself. For instance, you are playing baseball in a city park and someone is knocked unconscious by the ball. You make sure they are breathing, you immobilize them and then wait for the paramedics to arrive.

If you are in the wilderness two days from the nearest town and one of your party is knocked out by a falling rock and you smell smoke which suggests a wildfire is coming towards you, you have a different set of issues to deal with. Sometimes you have to take actions that you would not take if you were close to help. It is better to get the patient out of danger than to stay put and die in a wildfire.

If you or one of your group is injured, the nature of the injury will generally determine whether you stay in place or go. Minor injuries can be treated and should not impede progress. Serious injuries such as broken limbs, spinal and head injuries, problems caused by extreme conditions (heat stroke/hypothermia) and severe wounds need immediate and specific attention. Only after treatment can a decision be made about whether to stay or evacuate. In most cases, it is better to evacuate rapidly if the patient has life threatening injuries rather than stay put in the hope of an early rescue.

If the person is unconscious – check the scene (is it safe), then use **ABCDE** to assess patient's condition

A – Roll patient face-up and use head-tilt method to open **Airway**.

B – Look, listen and feel for movement and normal **Breathing.** If no breathing, start CPR or rescue breathing.

C – **Circulation**. Check for pulse and severe bleeding. If no pulse start CPR, if severe bleeding, expose wound and apply pressure.

D – Look for **Disability** from damage to spine. If damage suspected, control patient's head.

E – Assess **Environment.** Does patient need treatment/protection from extreme conditions.

If patient is conscious, check for alertness /responsiveness, medical history, what led up to the injury, then do a DOTS physical exam

D – Deformity – sign of damage to spine or limbs,

O – Open injuries – treat accordingly

T – Tenderness

S – Swelling -

Basic treatments

Abdominal illness – keep patient hydrated and on bland diet

Abrasions – clean wound, apply antibiotic and cover with sterile dressing

Altitude sickness – descend to lower altitude

Anaphylaxis (severe allergic reaction) – assist patient with epinephrine if available or oral antihistamine

Bites and Stings – remove bee stingers by gently scraping skin with the edge of a knife blade. Many venomous snakes when disturbed will administer a phantom bite – that is they bite you with their fangs but do not inject any venom. If venom is injected you will know about it in a few minutes with pain and swelling.

Poisonous snake bites on arm or leg – place bands about 2 inches above and below bite tight enough to prevent flow of blood around affected area but not tight enough to interfere with circulation. Animal bites and non-venomous snake bites - clean wound and cover with sterile dressing.

Natural insect repellants: citronella grass,

Interesting point: In the U.S. there are about 14,000 venomous snake bites every year however, only five or so of these people die as a result.

Bleeding and wound care –

Arterial blood (pumped from the heart) is bright red and a cut usually spurts or gushes while venous blood (going back to the heart) is dark red and has a steady flow.

Apply direct pressure long enough to staunch bleeding then wash wound, apply antibiotic ointment, cover with sterile dressing and secure. If wound is in a limb try to raise cut area so it is higher than the heart. For large open wounds that continue to bleed pack with a pressure dressing, apply antibiotic, cover and bandage. Suture if necessary. For neck wounds gently pinch wound to stop bleeding. For head wounds, cover with bulky dressing until bleeding stops, wash wound and secure sterile dressings in place.

Blisters – Clean area, use a sterilized needle to puncture side of blister to let fluid out, cover with moleskin.

Many years ago I was part of a group that spent ten days trekking through the Massif Central in France to open up a new long distance trail. The terrain was mountainous, the ground was hard and the weather broke heat records. So this picture was a typical nightly sight. We stopped for the day, pitched tents, took off our boots and socks and treated our blisters.

Brain and head injuries – Control any bleeding and stabilize patient's head. Monitor condition constantly.

Burns- Cool area with lots of cold water, remove clothing/jewelry in area. For first degree burns (small superficial burns)- wash area, apply antibiotic and cover with sterile dressing

For second and third degree burns (large/deep, severe burns) – cover burned area with loose sterile dressings, take steps to minimize shock, dehydration and hypothermia.

Chest wounds – stabilize rib fractures without restricting breathing. For sucking chest wound apply dressing taped down on three sides. If patient has difficulty breathing, insert gloved finger into wound to try to relieve pressure.

Ear injuries – Use cooking oil to flush insects/other objects out of ear.

Fractures – Clean any wound and then splint the patient. Use branches wrapped in clothing for padded splints. Immobilize a broken leg by strapping it to the good one.

Frostbite – apply gentle warmth to affected area (must be warm not hot). Never rub affected area with snow as it will do more damage or sit the patient by a fire to thaw out.

Heart attack – help patient self-administer aspirins/nitroglycerin if able to do so.

Heat exposure– There are several phases of heat exposure starting with heat syncope and heat cramps to heat exhaustion and finally heat stroke which can be fatal. Heat syncope often occurs after you have been sitting out in the open in the sun and then suddenly rise. You may feel dizzy or even faint. Recovery is usually swift once the person is allowed to lie down and rest in the shade. Heat cramps normally affect the abdomen and limbs and should be a tell-tale sign that something is wrong. Heat exhaustion manifests itself next with headaches, sweating and nausea. By the time you stop sweating you have probably got heat stroke. Your pulse quickens, your skins feels hot, you become delirious and then sink into unconsciousness.

Recognize the symptoms. If you start to cramp, stop whatever you are doing, find shelter from the sun and drink water. For heat exhaustion, find shelter from the sun, loosen clothing and drink small quantities of water at regular intervals (every 3-5 minutes). For heat stroke you really need someone to help you because you will be either delirious or unconscious. The first priority is to get the patient into the shade, loosen clothing, splash with water and administer small amounts of water supplemented with salts to replace lost fluids.

Hypothermia – You don't just get hypothermia in cold climates. If you are cold, tired and wet you can get hypothermia – even in Florida, especially if there is a wind chill factor. Symptoms – you start shivering as your body loses heat which leads to confusion irrational decision making (like taking off clothes because you think you are hot), followed by unconsciousness if not treated and then death. Normal body temperature is around 98.6. It only takes a drop in core body temp of three degrees for the patient to have difficulty speaking and lose coordination. Below 95 degrees a person is considered to have hypothermia. To avoid it – stay warm and dry. To treat it - remove patient from cold, remove wet clothing, insulate in blankets, rub patient's body to stimulate circulation and provide warm drinks. Do not rewarm the patient too rapidly.

Nosebleeds – Have patient lean forward and pinch just below bridge of nose for 10 minutes.

Shock – Symptoms are paleness, sweating, trembling and thirst. Determine cause of shock, keep patient warm and calm and do not allow to get dehydrated.

Spinal injuries – immobilize head, neck and back. Keep patient still and do not move – unless you have no other choice.

Sprains and strains – RICE - **Rest** injured area, **Immobilize** area, apply **Cold** to area, **Elevate** injured area above heart if possible. Splint the injured area is you need to be mobile.

Ticks – if traveling in tick country always stop and check yourself and others you are traveling with for these unwanted but fascinating guests. A female tick can survive for up to five years before finding a host to feed on. Use tweezers to grasp the mouth parts attached to your skin (do not grasp the tick's body) and remove.

Tooth injuries – use resin/sand for temporary fillings. For knocked out teeth, rinse and replace in socket without touching the root.

Tourniquets – Use only on arms and legs and only if blood loss is uncontrollable by direct pressure. Apply four inch wide strip 2 inches above wound (but not over a joint and never over the wound) and tighten using stick until bleeding stops. Note time. Release every 15-20 minutes to restore some blood flow and assess.

Medicinal Plants

For centuries, wild plants and herbs have been used to treat ailments in the countryside and some of these remedies can still be very useful today. The leaves of blackberries for instance can be used to treat diarrhea, dandelion leaves are a natural diuretic and plantain leaves – chewed to soften them up – can be rubbed on insect bites to relieve the swelling and pain. The resin from the pine tree when mixed with a little sand can make an effective temporary tooth filling. Beautyberry leaves provide a natural insect repellant while dog fennel can relieve the itching from bites and poison ivy rash.

Beauty berry – rub leaves on skin for effective insect repellent (bunches of lemon grass and dried cattails also act as insect repellant)

Dock leaves – cut leaves into strips and use as astringent bandage

Dog fennel – run on skin to stop itching from stings and bites

Florida betony – infuse leaves in hot water for relief of headaches

Hercules club – leaves infused in tea relieves toothache

Spanish moss – infused in hot water produces anti-bacterial drink

Turkey tail fungi – anti-microbial, anti-oxidant, anti-malerial

Usnea – natural antiseptic

Wild mint – chew or infuse leaves for antiseptic properties

Willow twigs – chew young twigs to combat headaches (contains salicin – an ingredient in aspirin), tea made from inner bark reduces fever

Yarrow leaves placed on wound stop bleeding.

Medicinal Preparations

Tea: Steep in hot water

Infusion: Soaking leaves and/or flowers in either hot or cold water. Cold infusions may need several hours.

Tincture: Plant extracts combined with alcohol (often vodka) left to stand in a jar for 2-3 weeks, with frequent shaking, before being strained and bottled.

Decoction: Usually refers to root, bark or seeds and involves slow simmering

Poultice: An external moist application applied to a wound or affected area i.e. rash. The poultice is prepared by crushing plant material to release saps and juices. In some cases the plant parts i.e. leaves can be chewed to soften and moisten them first.

Wash: A tea or infusion for external application.

Chapter Eight. Orientation & Navigation

Even if you do not have a map or compass and the battery of your smart phone with the GPS app has died, you should always be able to orient yourself. There are several techniques for locating north and that might be enough to help you navigate to safety. You can also find out what time of day it is and use the stars to navigate at night.

Orientation
Finding north – use a watch during day and the Big Dipper at night.

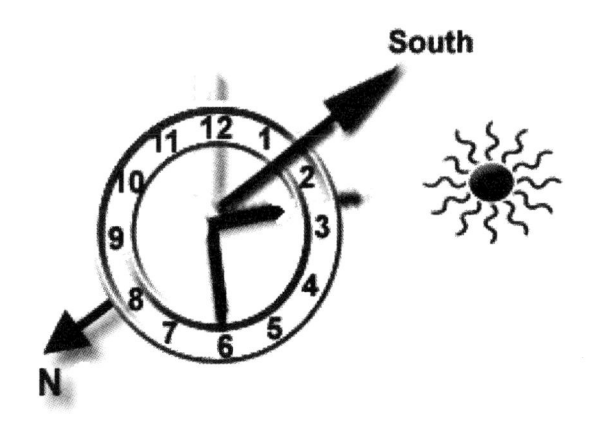

If you have an analog watch point the hour hand at the sun and then draw an imaginary line from the center of the watch bisecting the angle between the hour hand and noon which will point to south.

If you have a digital watch simply draw a watch face in the earth so that the hour hand is pointing to the sun.

On a starry night in the northern hemisphere it is easy to identify the seven stars that make up the Plow (also known as the Big Dipper). There are five stars that make up the handle of the Plow and two stars that make up the blade. The two blade stars are also known as the 'pointers' because if you follow the direction they are pointing, they will lead you to the North Star (Polaris).

Use a stick and follow the shadow which moves from west to east.
Find a clearing and place a straight stick about three feet long in the ground. Mark the end of the shadow – this will always be west. Wait ten to fifteen minutes until the shadow has moved and mark the end of the new shadow. Draw a line between the two marks and you will have a west-east axis from which you can locate north.

Telling time

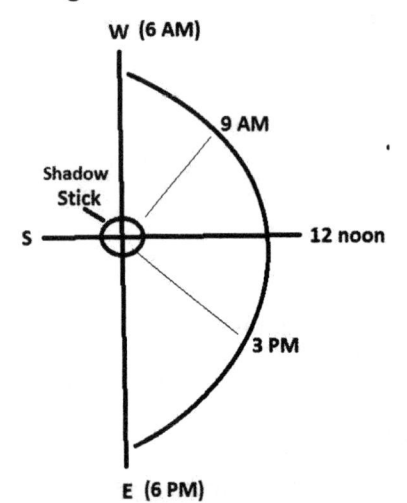

If you don't have a watch but have located north you can scratch out a 12 hour clock on the ground. Orient it so that 6 am is pointing to the west and 6 pm to the east. North will show noon. You can then divide these sections up equally to give you the in between hours. Place a stick in the ground in the center of the clock and its shadow will tell you what time it is.

Makeshift magnet – Stroke pin/needle etc. in one direction against synthetic cloth 20 - 30 times. Place on leaf in dish of water and pin will turn to point to magnetic north.

Use sun and moon – the moon is always opposite the sun.

If moon rises before sun sets, then the illuminated side faces west. If moon rises after midnight, the illuminated side faces east.

If there is a quarter moon, draw an imaginary straight line through the two tips and follow this until it hits the horizon. That point marks north in the northern hemisphere and south if you are in the southern hemisphere.

Tips: Climb a tree or high point to look for landmarks.

Follow rivers and waterways downstream –they often lead to civilization

Power lines always lead somewhere so follow them as a last resort.

Weather Forecasting

With mobile phones, pocket radios and GPS devices it is easy to keep in touch with the latest weather forecasts and that is important if you are in the countryside – especially in remote areas. Knowing what the weather is likely to do can allow you to set up camp ahead of a storm or if you are in the hills, descend to lower ground for safety.

However, well before we had all these hi-tech communication gadgets, country folks were able to predict – reasonably accurately – what the weather was going to do from seeing what was going on around them – and many of these observations still hold true today.

If you are camping in the country, find a large pine cone and keep it near the tent. An open cone indicates dry weather but if it closes up, it is probably going to rain. If you are neat the coast, seaweed can also be a good weather forecaster. If the seaweed feels dry to the touch the weather is likely to be dry, if the seaweed feels moist, it is going to be wet. The scientific explanation for this is that the seaweed reacts to changes in humidity so low humidity indicates dry weather and vice versa.

A red sky at night, a mist at dawn or heavy early morning dew all predict a warm day ahead. When cows are sitting or bunched together in the corner of a field it means rain is on its way. Also, cows don't like rain on their faces so if they are all sitting down and facing the same way, the rain is probably going to come from the other direction. Bees also dislike rain and so a stream of bees heading back to their hives is a sure sign of impending wet weather.

Another general rule of thumb is "Rain before seven, fine before eleven".

Bats are usually silent when they fly so when they squeak on the wing it is likely to rain quite soon. Gnats bite more if wet weather is on its way – although that is little consolation and a bug spray is still a good idea. Gnats also like to swarm in the open if the weather is fine but if rain threatens they stay in the shade.

In scores of ways, the animals, birds and flowers can help us predict the weather and tell us whether we will need our waterproofs. Wild marigolds open very wide if the day is set to be fine but don't open at all if rain is imminent. The scarlet pimpernel closes its small red flowers when it senses approaching rain, as do dandelions and daisies. When the flowers open again you know it is set to be fair for some time.

Swallows soar high in the sky hunting for insects in fine weather but fly much lower if the weather is changing and rain is coming. As pressure falls insects are unable to fly high. Geese fly high if it going to be fine but low when a storm is coming. Many songbirds also warn us of approaching wet weather. Blackbirds, robins and thrushes sing from the tops of the trees when it is going to stay fine, but sing from the lower branches if it is going to rain.

Spiders sense the approach of stormy weather and rush about spinning extra strands to hold their web in place.

Several species of tree – sycamore, poplar and lime - are also great predictors of wet weather. Many turn their leaves so that the lighter undersides are visible. The scientific reason for this is that as the moisture content in the atmosphere increases, the leaf stalks become moist and twist, turning the leaf over.

Beech trees are rarely struck by lightning (no one knows why) but if caught out in a storm look for a beech tree to shelter under.

When rooks leave their nests at dawn and fly off in a straight line, the day will be fine. When they leave later and take a zigzag course, it is going to be wet and if they stay at home, strong winds are likely.

The clouds can also help us make accurate weather forecasts. A mackerel sky means that any rain will be light and quickly over. Thin and wispy cirrus clouds are a sign of fair weather. Altocumulus clouds in the summer warn of approaching thunderstorms while nimbostratus clouds will bring rain.

As you sit round the campfire look up into the night sky and find out what the weather has in store for you the next day. A watery moon indicates approaching rain while a clear moon means a fine day ahead although in winter this could also mean a frost. Even the color of the moon tells us something – a pale moon means it is going to rain, a red moon is forecasting winds and a white moon tells us that the day ahead will be dry.

Always pay attention to what the animals and birds are doing, especially if you are camping in remote areas. Deer and highland cattle will make their way down to lower ground if they sense incoming bad weather so if you are hiking in the hills, follow their example and then seek shelter.

Did you Know? If you don't have a pen or it runs dry, you can always use a dandelion to make some notes. The clear sap that comes from the stem is like invisible ink. It may be a little difficult to see (or not to see) what you are writing, but when the 'ink' dries, the writing becomes legible like magic.

Signaling

If you need to signal for help it means that you are in trouble and that is exactly why you need to tell someone before you set out where you are going, what route you plan to take and when you expect to be back. Hopefully, if you do not return on time that person will notify the authorities and a search will be mounted for you.

There are several ways to attract attention in an emergency. Obviously the best way is to use your mobile phone to summon the cavalry but what if you have no signal.

Be seen and be heard

Fires – make lots of smoke using damp wood and vegetation. Wet bark generates lots of smoke.

Mirrors – use signal mirrors, aluminum cup, belt buckle or the blade of a knife – they can be seen by aircraft 50-75 miles away. Use the moon at night. Use a signaling mirror that has a sighting hole so that you can flash it directly at the aircraft. When signaling move the mirror back and forth – don't direct the light straight into the pilot's eyes

Beacons/markers – build in a clearing using logs, branches, clothing, stones, or scraping away earth. Large **X** indicates "Help – Can't Proceed", large **XI** means "Need Doctor". Signals should be at least 18 feet long and three feet wide to be seen from air. If there are no materials to build the cross, spread out your emergency space blanket.

Whistles, shouting - You can call out to people you see in the distance but they may not hear you if it is windy. A better way is to blow a whistle. The international distress signal is SOS which in Morse Code is dot, dot, dot, dash, dash, dash, dot, dot, dot. Use the whistle to repeatedly send out your SOS – three short blasts, three long blasts and then three short blasts again. Or just repeat at intervals three short blasts which is also generally recognized as a help signal.

Chapter Nine. Fishing & Trapping

If trying to move silently after prey, put a pair of thick socks over your boots or trainers.

Bird eggs are a great source of nutrition during the nesting season. Don't take all the eggs, if you leave one or two in each nest, the birds may lay more.

Trap birds, animals and fish, clean and eat as soon as possible.

Roast young birds, boil old birds

Fish eating birds tend to have 'fishy' skins so are best skinned before cooking

Fish can be wrapped in leaves, baked in embers or stewed

Many creatures can be eaten raw – snakes (not the head), fish and insects.

Even worms can provide a nutritious meal. After digging them up drop them in a container of water. They will naturally purge themselves and you can then eat them raw or add them to stews.

Boil shellfish and eat, boil turtles until the shell comes off and then roast

Skinning and gutting

Whenever skinning and gutting take care not to cut through any organs or glands so as not to contaminate the meat.

Large animals – lay the animal on the ground belly up – ideally on a slope so that the head is upslope. Make a cut from below the tail to the throat and separate cuts down the inside of each leg – from the top of the leg to the ankle joint or equivalent. You then have to get your hands in under the cuts and tug the hide off. It takes some effort. Once removed, make a cut from the sex organs to the chest - taking care not to puncture any organs. Use a knife to cut around the sex organs and remove together with all other organs in the abdomen in the chest cavity, including windpipe and gullet. Separate the edible organs from the non-edible. The advantage of the slope is that the waste organs once removed, can be placed downslope to reduce the chance of contaminating the meat. Another great use of the black garbage bags is that all the waste can be contained inside ready for disposal.

In hot weather, the meat will have to be eaten quite quickly but in cooler climates the animal can be hung for a few days before spoiling provided it is protected from other animals and insects.

Remember: Tendons, sinews and strips of hide can all be used for cordage.

Small animals – make a cut around the middle of the back from one side to the other. Slide two or three fingers of one hand into the incision so they face the head and use the other hand to insert two or three fingers facing the tail and pull the skin off. Then remove the head and clean.

Gut reptiles and amphibians and roast in fire embers - skin frogs first. Small lizards can be cooked on a stick over the fire.

Cooking

You can boil large pieces of meat to tenderize them before roasting or add them to the stew pot and cook slowly. The offal – heart, liver, kidneys and brain are all edible as is the tongue – if skinned and slow boiled.

Small fish (less than four inches) can be cooked whole. Large fish should be gutted first. Always cook with the skin on as it contains valuable nutrients. Large fish can be impaled on a stick and cooked over the fire but there is always the danger they will break up and fall off. Boiling allows you to get the most nutritional value

Preserving meat

Cutting meat with the grain into thin strips allows it to be air dried if the weather is hot. Keep the drying meat out of the reach of animals and cover to keep insects away.

Taste

We'll all heard it before - ask someone what it tastes like and they say chicken. Now the scientists have discovered why.

Small critters (up to the size of a small dog) tend to taste like chicken because they all have similar muscle density and composition. Medium size critters (up the size of a large dog) tend to taste like pork, and large critters tend to taste like beef for the same reason.

Hunting

Like all outdoor skills, hunting takes a lot of practice and can expend a lot of time and energy. It may be macho charging off into the bush with a spear but it is not wise. Survival is all about conservation of energy and if it is easier to gather nuts and berries and eat salads and roasted roots that is what you should do.

If you are going to hunt, fish, birds and smaller animals and easier to take. Large animals are difficult to kill, they may fight back and they have to be lugged back to camp or butchered on the spot. And, as discussed earlier meat goes bad after a few days unless you can preserve it by drying or smoking. Even if you did catch a large animal you might have to throw a lot of the meat away.

It is best to hunt early morning or at dusk. It you are stalking an animal stay upwind and freeze if the animal looks your way. If waiting by a trap or regularly used watering hole, hide downwind.

Use a short forked branch to push into hollows in trees. By twisting it around you may snag a small critter inside. You can use smoke to flush out animals from their burrows but you will need a noose on the end of a pole to catch them as they emerge. The same device can also be used to catch nesting or roosting birds.

Tip: Squirrels usually hide as you approach by clinging to the side of the tree away from you. Stay where you are and throw a stone or piece of wood so that it lands on the squirrel's side. The squirrel will automatically move round to your side of the tree and if you are quick enough you can catch it with a noose on a pole.

Tracking

Being able to recognize tracks and scat and having some knowledge of critters' habits will make it a lot easier to find and catch them. Animals have different gaits – some walk while others hop. Note below that some animals have four toes – like the bobcat, fox and coyote - while other have five toes - like the bears and raccoons. It is also useful to know the preferred habitats of different critters. If you know what animal you are hunting and where best to find them, you can prepare the right traps and snares.

Bobcat	American Alligator	Florida Black Bear

Grey Fox	White-Tailed Deer	Wild Turkey

Snares - you can buy wire snares or make your own. Wire is best because the critter can't bite through it, but if you are using a noose that will tighten once the critter's head is caught in it, strong twine will do.

Use a loop or noose attached firmly to a branch or stake and place near the animal's den or game trail. Then camouflage and obliterate your scent - human scent lingers for 3 days). Some snares have spring triggers that will tighten the noose but a simple drag noose works just as well. Once the animal's head is caught its struggles tighten the noose.

Traps – setting multiple traps (tension traps/deadfall) increases your odds
Spearing – for fish, small animals and reptiles. A diagonal tip stronger than a pointed tip. Harden further by holding over flames.

Bird poles - at the end of a long pole attach a slip noose. This method requires a lot of patience but if once slipped over the neck of a roosting bird the noose will immediately tighten and you have supper.

Rodent traps - dig a round hole about 20 inches deep with walls narrower at the top than the bottom. Place a large piece of bark over the hole supported about one inch off the ground by twigs and small stones. Small rodents will seek shelter under the bark and then fall into the hole from which they cannot escape. Always check out what is in the trap before reaching down into the hole – you don't want a rat or snake bite.

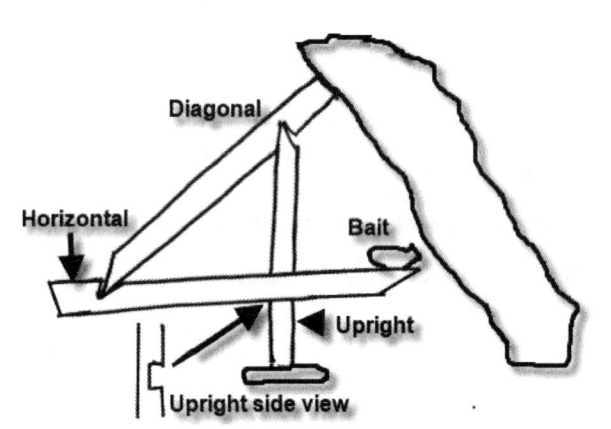

Deadfall traps – a deadfall trap involves a heavy object (a rock or tree limb) set at a 45 degree angle to the ground and held up by a figure four trigger consisting of three sticks –diagonal, upright and horizontal as in the diagram below. One end of the diagonal supports the heavy object while the other rests in a notch on the horizontal stick. The diagonal is held loosely in place by the upright while the horizontal stick provides the trigger. All the pieces need to fit together loosely so that they will ready fall apart when the trap is sprung/The bait is placed on the end of the horizontal stick under the heavy object. When the animal takes the bait, the horizontal stick is dislodged and falls to the ground followed by the upright while the diagonal flips out of the way and the heavy weight crashes down. Always stand the upright on a hard flat object so that it is not pressed into the ground preventing it from falling when the trigger is released. A good rule of thumb is that the deadfall should be at least two times heavier than the prey you are intending to kill.

Fishing

Your survival kits should contain fish hooks or items that can substitute for them. You can also fashion basic fish hooks from bone, shell or wood. Freshwater lakes and streams can provide lots of other edibles beside fish – snails, mollusks, frogs, crawfish and crabs. If you bait a hook with a small fish and leave it just above the water level, a bird might come and grab it and become snagged.

Fish spear.
You can lash your knife to the end of a long pole and use this or you can cut a straight branch and make a split at one end and then use a small piece of wood to drive the two ends apart. These ends can then be sharpened and you have an effecting fishing spear. Don't lunge at the fish because you will always fail. Place the end of the spear in the water and then try to skewer the fish as you push it down onto the river bed. Once impaled, reach down to secure the fish rather than lift the spear out of the water as the fish will likely get away.

Fish traps – use stakes in streams, rivers and near lake shores to corral fish. Funnel fish into the narrow entrance of the trap.

When fishing or spear fishing make sure your back is not to the sun because if it is it will cast a large shadow in front of you scaring away the fish.

Chapter Ten. Hiking and Survival Kits

There is a difference between your regular hiking/backpacking gear and your survival kit. In fact, you should have several emergency kits – one for the house, one for the car and one to keep with you even if you are just going for a quick stroll in the woods.

My survival kit weighs just over two pounds and was put together for less than $20 using mostly everyday household objects yet I can use it to survive in the wilderness for as long as I need to. More about this later.

Always consider your clothing part of your survival kit. Chosen carefully, they should keep you dry and when necessary, warm – two of the critical elements of survival.

Lightweight, loose, quick drying clothes are best. Long sleeved shirts are better than short sleeves – you can always roll the sleeves up. Trousers are better than shorts affording more protection against thorns, insect bites and so on.

Lightweight windproof, waterproof outer shell jacket and trousers are also a must and allow you to layer up or down depending on the weather. Outer shells not only protect from rain and cold, they will protect you from relentless sun as well. When you are baking from the heat taking clothes off doesn't cool you down it simply exposes more skin to the sun. Covering up with light clothing will help you cool down.

Boots offering ankle support are better than trainers and sandals may be OK around the campsite but are not suitable on the trail and especially in rough terrain.

A hat is a good idea whether it is hot or cold – you can lose half your body heat through the head - and always pack gloves.

Survival Kit

Your emergency kit should allow you to shelter, stay warm, light a fire, purify water and attract the attention of rescuers. I don't recommend buying ready assembled-survival kits – the quality of most is dire and I wouldn't want to trust my life with much of the equipment provided. It is much better to put together your own kit. Essential items could include:

Basic first aid kit including tweezers, plastic magnifying glass

Sewing kit and hooks (for repairs, improvised fishing gear and sutures)

Compass (and know how to use it)

Emergency space blanket

Flashlight

ID (some sort of personal identification)

Knife – multi blade (with sharp blade, scissors, corkscrew, mini saw and can opener)

Water purification tablets

Waterproof matches and fire steel

Whistle – the new Coastguard whistles can be heard up to two miles away and can even be blown under water

Six-strand parachute cord

Signaling mirror

Two large black garbage bags

Several smaller Ziploc-type plastic bags

Hiking Gear

One day trips

You need your walking clothes and footwear plus a day pack containing map, raingear, snacks and emergency rations, water bottle and a lightweight emergency blanket.

Don't forget personal items such as, lip salve, suntan cream, insect repellent, and toilet paper. If you plan on cooking a meal while on the trail you will need a lightweight backpack stove and pot plus pre-packaged meal ingredients.

(Box)

Full size emergency blankets when packed are the size of a pack of cards and weigh under 2ozs. They are gold colored on one side and silver on the other – one side to keep the heat in and the other to act as a reflector which could be spotted by searchers. If someone is injured unroll the blanket and wrap round the person to conserve as much energy as possible. If possible, cover the head and draw legs towards the chest to conserve body core temperature. For post-trauma shock, wrap the blanket around the victim and keep immobile and get medical help as soon as possible.

(end box)

Lightweight kit for varying lengths of stay

Tent or bivvy bag, sleeping bag, change of clothing,

Stove, cooking pots, pot grabber and mug together with fuel and basic utensils will have to be packed. Keep stove and fuel packed separately and away from the food.

Tip: Paint pot grabbers a bright color or bind with reflective tape so that you can easily spot them.

For longer trips, in addition to the above you will also need:

Another form of fire lighter (brightly colored lighter – so that if you drop it you will see it, or flint and steel)

Aluminum foil (can be used for cooking, shaped into a bowl to carry water, used to wrap wounds and a host of other things.)

Candles and/or lantern

Clothing - several changes of 'layer' (add layers if cold, remove layers if hot)

Extra batteries for flashlight (torch)

Hat

Headlight

Nylon rope 10m (30 feet)

Sandals or light weight trainers (to slip into when the boots come off)

Sewing kit (for basic repairs, emergency sutures!)

Socks and sock liners

Small roll of duct tape (for repairs)

Small trowel or very lightweight folding shovel

Toilet paper

Washing kit, towel and other personal hygiene requirements

Depending on the time of the year, you may also need:

Gloves

Insect repellant

Lip balm

Pack cover (a waterproof that slips over your pack to protect it from the rain)

Small hatchet/folding saw

Sunglasses

Sunscreen

Weather radio

Other optional items, depending on your interests, could be:

Binoculars (compact 7x24 for instance fit into a shirt pocket)

Camera and film/memory cards (and spare camera batteries)

Playing cards

Field Guides

Fishing rod and tackle

Journey log and pen

Paperback/ magazines (excellent tinder if lighting fires)

Wet wipes

My backpacking/survival kit

Backpack   Backpack and basic contents

My pack contains bivvy bag, aluminum pot, knife and survival kit.

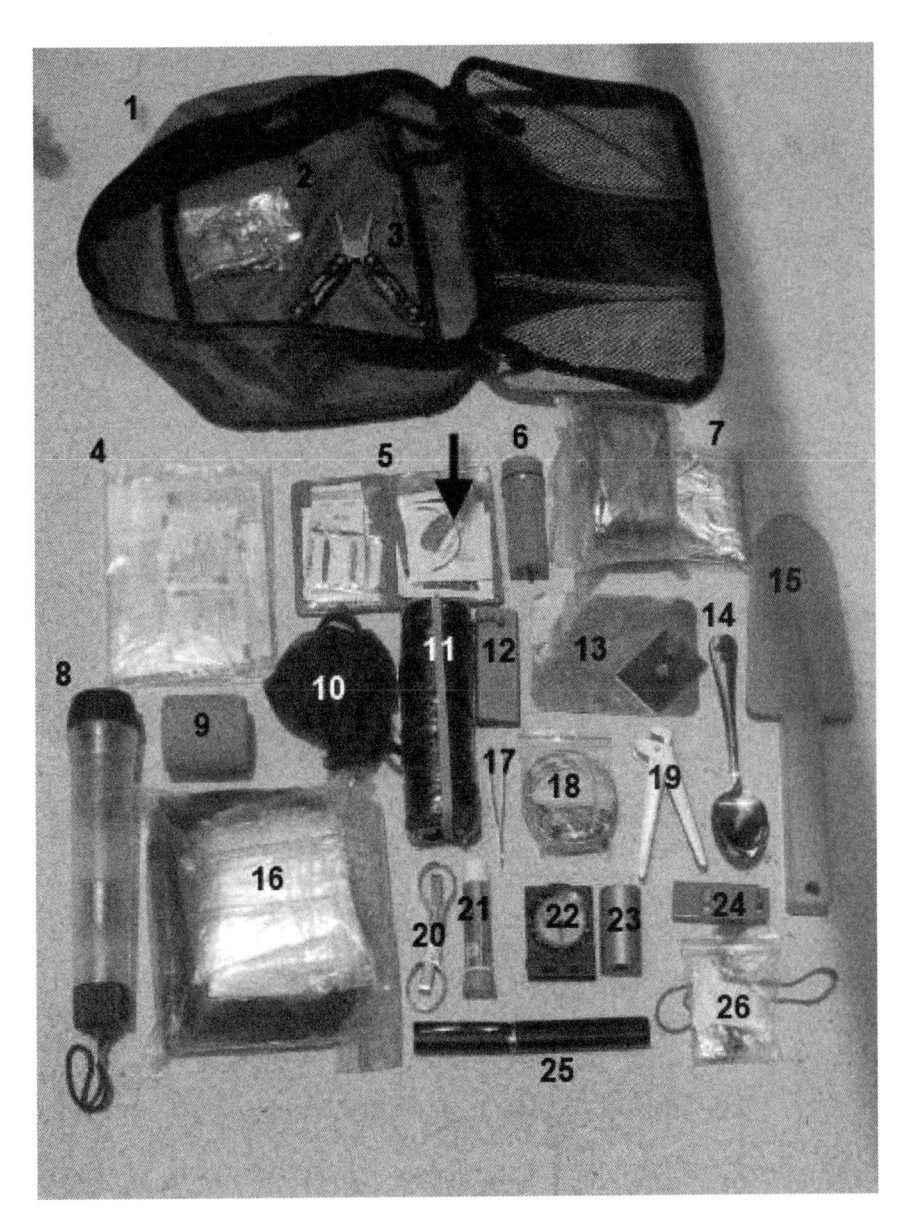

1. My survival bag – keeps it all together
2. Small animal spring loaded snares
3. Mini-multi-tool. Pliers are useful for removing fish hooks.
4. First aid pouch, Band-Aids, wipes

75

5. Sewing/repair kit, needles (can also be used for fishing). Arrow points to needle that can also be used for sutures (after sterlilizing)
6. Waterproof matches in waterproof container
7. Two space blankets (multiple uses – shelter, signaling, blanket etc.
8. Flashlight (activated by shaking – no batteries)
9. Elasticated bandage
10. Mosquito head protector
11. Six-strand parachute cord
12. Magnesium striker
13. Two signal mirrors – signaling and examining wounds behind your back
14. Metal spoon – for cooking, eating, cracking open nuts, mollusks.
15. Trowel – for foraging roots, digging latrine
16. Plastic bags (two large black garbage bags, several smaller clear bags) – multiple uses – poncho, sleeping bags, containers, wrapping and protecting wounds, solar stills, waterproofing shelters
17. Tweezers
18. Snares for larger animals
19. Ultra lightweight pot grab
20. Scissors
21. Instant glue – for repairs and closing up wounds
22. Compass
23. Duct tape – multiple uses
24. Whistle
25. Spare pair of glasses
26. Fishing line and hooks

Chapter Eleven. Natural Hazards

The following sections look at the many natural hazards that you might come across, how you can prepare for them and more important, how you can survive them.

Floods

Floods are among the most common hazards in the U.S. However, all floods are not alike. Riverine floods develop slowly, sometimes over a period of days. Flash floods can develop quickly, sometimes in just a few minutes, without any visible signs of rain. Flash floods often have a dangerous wall of roaring water that carries a deadly cargo of rocks, mud and other debris and can sweep away most things in its path. Overland flooding occurs outside a defined river or stream, such as when a levee is breached, but still can be destructive. Flooding can also occur from a dam break producing effects similar to flash floods.

Flood effects can be very local, impacting a neighborhood or community, or very large, affecting entire river basins and multiple states. Be aware of flood hazards no matter where you live, but especially if you live in a low-lying area, near water or downstream from a dam. Even very small streams, gullies, creeks, culverts, dry streambeds or low-lying ground that appear harmless in dry weather can flood. Every state is at risk from this hazard.

What to do Before a Flood

1. Know the terms used to describe flooding:
    - Flood Watch – Flooding is possible. Stay tuned to NOAA Weather Radio or commercial radio or television for information. Watches are issued 12 to 36 hours in advance of a possible flooding event.
    - Flash Flood Watch – Flash flooding is possible. Be prepared to move to higher ground. A flash flood could occur without any warning. Listen to NOAA Weather Radio or commercial radio or television for additional information.
    - Flood Warning – Flooding is occurring or will occur soon. If advised to evacuate, do so immediately.
    - Flash Flood Warning – A flash flood is occurring. Seek higher ground on foot immediately.

2. Ask local officials whether your property is in a flood-prone or high-risk area. (Remember that floods often occur outside high-risk areas.) Ask about official flood warning signals and what to do when you hear them. Also ask how you can protect your home from flooding.

3. Identify dams in your area and determine whether they pose a hazard to you.

4. Purchase a NOAA Weather Radio with battery backup and a tone-alert feature that automatically alerts you when a Watch or Warning is issued (tone alert is not available in some areas). Purchase a battery-powered commercial radio and extra batteries.

5. Be prepared to evacuate. Learn your community's flood evacuation routes and where to find high ground. See the "Evacuation" sections in this handbook.

6. Talk to your household about flooding. Plan a place to meet your household in case you are separated from one another in a disaster and cannot return home. Choose an out-of-town contact for everyone to call to say they are OK. In some emergencies, calling out-of-state is possible even when local phone lines are down.

7. Determine how you would care for household members who may live elsewhere but might need your help in a flood. Determine any special needs your neighbors might have.

8. Prepare to survive on your own for at least three days. Assemble a disaster supply kit. Keep a stock of food and extra drinking water. See the "Emergency Planning and Disaster Supplies" sections for more information.

9. Know how to shut off electricity, gas and water at main switches and valves. Know where gas pilot lights are located and how the heating system works.

10. Consider purchasing flood insurance:
- Flood losses are not covered under homeowners' insurance policies.
- FEMA manages the National Flood Insurance Program, which makes federally backed flood insurance available in communities that agree to adopt and enforce floodplain management ordinances to reduce future flood damage.
- Flood insurance is available in most communities through insurance agents.
- There is a 30-day waiting period before flood insurance goes into effect, so don't delay.
- Flood insurance is available whether the building is in or out of the identified flood-prone area.

11. Consider options for protecting your property:

- Make a record of your personal property. Take photographs or videotapes of your belongings. Store these documents in a safe place.
- Keep insurance policies, deeds, property records and other important papers in a safe place away from your home.
- Avoid building in a floodplain unless you elevate and reinforce your home.
- Elevate furnace, water heater, and electric panel to higher floors or the attic if they are susceptible to flooding.
- Install "check valves" in sewer traps to prevent floodwater from backing up into the drains of your home.
- Construct barriers, such as levees, berms and floodwalls to stop floodwater from entering the building.
- Seal walls in basements with waterproofing compounds to avoid seepage.
- Call your local building department or emergency management office for more information.

What to do During a Flood
1. Be aware of flash flooding. If there is any possibility of a flash flood, move immediately to higher ground. Do not wait for instructions to move.
2. Listen to radio or television stations for local information.
3. Be aware of streams, drainage channels, canyons and other areas known to flood suddenly. Flash floods can occur in these areas with or without such typical warning signs as rain clouds or heavy rain.
4. If local authorities issue a flood watch, prepare to evacuate:
    - Secure your home. If you have time, tie down or bring outdoor equipment and lawn furniture inside. Move essential items to the upper floors.
    - If instructed, turn off utilities at the main switches or valves. Disconnect electrical appliances. Do not touch electrical equipment if you are wet or standing in water.
    - Fill the bathtub with water in case water becomes contaminated or services cut off. Before filling the tub, sterilize it with a diluted bleach solution.

5. Do not walk through moving water. Six inches of moving water can knock you off your feet. If you must walk in a flooded area, walk where the water is not moving. Use a stick to check the firmness of the ground in front of you.
6. Do not drive into flooded areas. Six inches of water will reach the bottom of most passenger cars causing loss of control and possible stalling. A foot of

water will float many vehicles. Two feet of water will wash away almost all vehicles. If floodwaters rise around your car, abandon the car and move to higher ground, if you can do so safely. You and your vehicle can be quickly swept away as floodwaters rise.
7. See the "Evacuation" section for important information.

What to do After a Flood
1. Avoid floodwaters. The water may be contaminated by oil, gasoline or raw sewage. The water may also be electrically charged from underground or downed power lines.
2. Avoid moving water. Moving water only six inches deep can sweep you off your feet.
3. Be aware of areas where floodwaters have receded. Roads may have weakened and could collapse under the weight of a car.
4. Stay away from downed power lines and report them to the power company.
5. Stay away from designated disaster areas unless authorities ask for volunteers.
6. Return home only when authorities indicate it is safe. Stay out of buildings if they are surrounded by floodwaters. Use extreme caution when entering buildings. There may be hidden damage, particularly in foundations.
7. Consider your family's health and safety needs:
- Wash hands frequently with soap and clean water if you come in contact with floodwaters.
- Throw away food that has come in contact with floodwaters.
- Listen for news reports to learn whether the community's water supply is safe to drink.
- Listen to news reports for information about where to get assistance for housing, clothing and food.
- Seek necessary medical care at the nearest medical facility.

8. Service damaged septic tanks, cesspools, pits, and leaching systems as soon as possible. Damaged sewage systems are serious health hazards.
9. Contact your insurance agent. If your policy covers your situation, an adjuster will be assigned to visit your home. To prepare:
- Take photos of your belongings and your home or videotape them.
- Separate damaged and undamaged belongings.
- Locate your financial records.
- Keep detailed records of cleanup costs.

10. If your residence has been flooded obtain a copy of "Repairing Your Flooded Home" from the local American Red Cross chapter.

11. See the "Recovering From Disaster" sections for more information.

Hurricanes

A hurricane is a type of tropical cyclone, the generic term for a low-pressure system that generally forms in the tropics. The ingredients for a hurricane include a pre-existing weather disturbance, warm tropical oceans, moisture, and relatively light winds aloft. A typical cyclone is accompanied by thunderstorms, and in the Northern Hemisphere, a counterclockwise circulation of winds near the earth's surface. Tropical cyclones are classified as follows:

Tropical Depression - An organized system of clouds and thunderstorms with a defined surface circulation and maximum sustained winds of 38 mph (33 knots) or less. Sustained winds are defined as one-minute average wind measured at about 33 feet above the surface.

Tropical Storm - An organized system of strong thunderstorms with a defined surface circulation and maximum sustained winds of 39-73 mph (34-63 knots).

Hurricane - An intense tropical weather system of strong thunderstorms with a well-defined surface circulation and maximum sustained winds of 74 mph (64 knots) or higher. All Atlantic and Gulf of Mexico coastal areas are subject to hurricanes and tropical storms. Although rarely struck by hurricanes, parts of the Southwest United States and the Pacific Coast experience heavy rains and floods each year from hurricanes spawned off Mexico. The Atlantic hurricane season lasts from June through November with the peak season from mid-August to late October.

As we all have seen, hurricanes can cause catastrophic and deadly damage to coastlines and several hundred miles inland. Winds can exceed 155 miles per hour. Hurricanes and tropical storms can also spawn tornadoes and microbursts, create a surge along the coast, and cause extensive damage due to inland flooding from trapped water.

Tornadoes most often occur in thunderstorms embedded in rain bands well away from the center of the hurricane; however, they also occur near the eye-wall. Typically, tornadoes produced by tropical cyclones are relatively weak and short-lived but still pose a threat.

A storm surge is a huge dome of water pushed on-shore by hurricane and tropical storm winds. Storm surges can reach 25 feet high and be 50-100 miles wide. Storm tide is a combination of the storm surge and the normal tide (i.e., a 15-foot storm surge combined with a 2-foot normal high tide over the mean sea level creates a 17-foot storm tide). These phenomena cause severe erosion and extensive damage to coastal areas.

Despite improved warnings and a decrease in the loss of life, property damage continues to rise because an increasing number of people are living or vacationing near coastlines. Those in hurricane-prone areas need to be prepared for hurricanes and tropical storms.

Hurricanes are classified into five categories based on their wind speed, central pressure and damage potential. Category Three and higher are considered major hurricanes, though Category One and Two are still extremely dangerous and warrant your full attention.

Inland/Freshwater Flooding from Hurricanes
Hurricanes can produce widespread torrential rains. Floods are the deadly and destructive result. Excessive rain can also trigger landslides or mud slides, especially in mountainous regions. Flash flooding can occur due to the intense rainfall. Flooding on rivers and streams may persist for several days or more after the storm.

The speed of the storm and the geography beneath the storm are the primary factors regarding the amount of rain produced. Slow moving storms and tropical storms moving into mountainous regions tend to produce more rain.

Between 1970 and 1999, more people lost their lives from freshwater flooding associated with land-falling tropical cyclones than from any other weather hazard related to tropical cyclones.

What to do Before a Hurricane
1. Know the difference between "Watches" and "Warnings:"
    - Hurricane/Tropical Storm Watch – Hurricane/tropical storm conditions are possible in the specified area, usually within 36 hours.
    - Hurricane/Tropical Storm Warning – Hurricane/tropical storm conditions are expected in the specified area, usually within 24 hours.

- Short Term Watches and Warnings – warnings provide detailed information on specific hurricane threats, such as flash floods and tornadoes.

Saffir-Simpson Hurricane Scale

Scale Category	Sustained winds	Damage	Surge
1	74-95 MPH	Minimal: Untied mobile homes, vegetation & signs	4-5 feet
2	96-110	Moderate: All mobile homes, roofs, small crafts, flooding.	6-8
3	111-130	Extensive: Small buildings, low-lying roads cut-off.	9-12
4	131-155	Extreme. Roofs destroyed, trees down, roads cut off, mobile homes destroyed, beach homes flooded.	13-18
5	Over 155	Catastrophic. Most buildings over 18 feet destroyed. Vegetation destroyed, major roads cut off, homes flooded	Over 18

2. Listen for local radio or television weather forecasts. Purchase a NOAA Weather Radio with battery backup and a tone-alert feature that automatically alerts you when a Watch or Warning is issued (tone alert is not available in some areas). Purchase a battery-powered commercial radio and extra batteries, because the media will be broadcasting information on other events as well.

3. Ask your local emergency management office about community evacuation plans relating to your neighborhood. Learn evacuation routes. Determine where you would go and how you would get there if you needed to evacuate. Sometimes alternate routes are desirable.

4. Talk to your household about hurricane issues. Create a household disaster plan. Plan to meet at a place away from your residence in case you are separated. Choose an out-of-town contact for everyone to call to say they are safe.

5. Determine the needs of your household members who may live elsewhere but need your help in a hurricane. Consider the special needs of neighbors, such as people who are disabled or those with limited sight or vision problems.

6. Prepare to survive on your own for at least three days. Assemble a disaster supply kit. Keep a stock of food and extra drinking water. See the "Emergency Planning and Disaster Supplies" and "Evacuation" sections for more information.

7. Make plans to secure your property. Permanent storm shutters offer the best protection for windows. A second option is to board up windows with 5/8" marine plywood, cut to fit and ready to install. Tape does not prevent windows from breaking.

8. Learn how to shut off utilities and where gas pilots and water mains are located.

9. Have your home inspected for compliance with local building codes. Many of the roofs destroyed by hurricanes have not been constructed or retrofitted according to building codes. Installing straps or additional clips to securely fasten your roof to the frame structure will substantially reduce roof damage.

10. Be sure trees and shrubs around your home are well trimmed. Dead limbs or trees could cause personal injury or property damage. Clear loose and clogged rain gutters and downspouts.

11. If you have a boat, determine where to secure it in an emergency.

12. Consider flood insurance. Purchase insurance well in advance – there is a 30-day waiting period before flood insurance takes effect.

13. Make a record of your personal property. Take photographs or videotapes of your belongings. Store these documents in a safe place.

What to do During a Hurricane Threat

1. Listen to radio or television newscasts. If a hurricane "Watch" is issued, you typically have 24 to 36 hours before the hurricane hits land.

2. Talk with household members. Make sure everyone knows where to meet and who to call, in case you are separated. Consider the needs of relatives and neighbors with special needs.

3. Secure your home. Close storm shutters. Secure outdoor objects or bring them indoors. Moor your boat if time permits.

4. Gather several days' supply of water and food for each household member. Water systems may become contaminated or damaged. Sterilize (with diluted bleach solution of one part bleach to 10 parts water) and fill the bathtub to ensure a supply of safe water in case you are unable or told not to evacuate. Refer to the "Shelter and Emergency Planning" and "Disaster Supplies" chapters for important information.

5. If you are evacuating, take your disaster supply kit with you to the shelter. Remember that alcoholic beverages and weapons are prohibited within shelters. Also, pets are not usually allowed in a public shelter due to health reasons. See the "Animals in Disasters" chapter and contact your local humane society for additional information.

6. Prepare to evacuate. Fuel your car – service stations may be closed after the storm. If you do not have a car, make arrangements for transportation with a friend or relative. Review evacuation routes. If instructed, turn off utilities at the main valves.

7. Evacuate to an inland location if:
- Local authorities announce an evacuation and you live in an evacuation zone.
- You live in a mobile home or temporary structure – they are particularly hazardous during hurricanes no matter how well fastened to the ground.
- You live in a high-rise. Hurricane winds are stronger at higher elevations.
- You live on the coast, on a floodplain near a river or inland waterway.
- You feel you are in danger.

8. When authorities order an evacuation:
- Leave immediately.
- Follow evacuation routes announced by local officials.
- Stay away from coastal areas, riverbanks and streams.
- Tell others where you are going.

9. If you are not required or are unable to evacuate, stay indoors during the hurricane and away from windows and glass doors. Keep curtains and blinds closed. Do not be fooled if there is a lull, it could be the eye of the storm – winds will pick up again.
- Turn off utilities if told to do so by authorities.
- If not instructed to turn off, turn the refrigerator to its coldest setting and keep closed.
- Turn off propane tanks.

10. In strong winds, follow these rules:

- Take refuge in a small interior room, closet or hallway.
- Close all interior doors. Secure and brace external doors.
- In a two-story residence, go to an interior first-floor room, such as a bathroom or closet.
- In a multiple-story building, go to the first or second floors and stay in interior rooms away from windows.
- Lie on the floor under a table or another sturdy object.

11. Avoid using the phone except for serious emergencies. Local authorities need first priority on telephone lines.
12. See the "Evacuation" sections for important information.

What to do After a Hurricane

1. Stay where you are if you are in a safe location until local authorities say it is safe to leave. If you evacuated the community, do not return to the area until authorities say it is safe to return.
2. Keep tuned to local radio or television stations for information about caring for your household, where to find medical help, how to apply for financial assistance, etc.
3. Drive only when necessary. Streets will be filled with debris. Roads may have weakened and could collapse. Do not drive on flooded or barricaded roads or bridges. Closed roads are for your protection. As little as six inches of water may cause you to lose control of your vehicle – two feet of water will carry most cars away.
4. Do not drink or prepare food with tap water until notified by officials that it is safe to do so.
5. Consider your family's health and safety needs. Be aware of symptoms of stress and fatigue. Keep your household together and seek crisis counseling if you have need.
6. Talk with your children about what has happened and how they can help during the recovery. Being involved will help them deal with the situation. Consider the needs of your neighbors. People often become isolated during hurricanes.
7. Stay away from disaster areas unless local authorities request volunteers. If you are needed, bring your own drinking water, food and sleeping gear.
8. Stay away from riverbanks and streams until potential flooding has passed. Do not allow children, especially under the age of 13, to play in flooded areas. There is a high risk of injury or drowning in areas that may appear safe.

9. Stay away from moving water. Moving water only six inches deep can sweep you off your feet. Standing water may be electrically charged from underground or downed power lines.
10. Stay away from downed power lines and report them to the power company. Report to local officials any broken gas, sewer or water mains.
11. Don't use candles or other open flames indoors. Use a flashlight to inspect damage.
12. Set up a manageable schedule to repair property.
13. Contact your insurance agent. An adjuster will be assigned to visit your home. To prepare:
- Take photos of your belongings and your home or videotape them.
- Separate damaged and undamaged belongings.
- Locate your financial records.
- Keep detailed records of cleanup costs.

14. Consider building a "Safe Room or Shelter" to protect your household. See the "Thunderstorms" sections for additional information in the "Tornadoes" section.
15. See the "Recovering From Disaster" section for more important information.

Thunderstorms

Thunderstorms are very common and affect great numbers of people each year. Despite their small size in comparison to hurricanes and winter storms, all thunderstorms are dangerous. Every thunderstorm produces lightning. Other associated dangers of thunderstorms include tornadoes, strong winds, hail, and flash flooding. Flash flooding is responsible for more fatalities – more than 140 annually – than any other thunderstorm-associated hazard.

Some thunderstorms do not produce rain that reaches the ground. These are generically referred to as dry thunderstorms and are most prevalent in the western United States. Known to spawn wildfires, these storms occur when there is a large layer of dry air between the base of the cloud and the ground. The falling raindrops evaporate, but lightning can still reach the ground.

What to do Before Thunderstorms Approach
1. Know the terms used by weather forecasters:

- Severe Thunderstorm Watch – Tells you when and where severe thunderstorms are likely to occur. Watch the sky and stay tuned to radio or television to know when warnings are issued.
- Severe Thunderstorm Warning – Issued when severe weather has been reported by spotters or indicated by radar. Warnings indicate imminent danger to life and property to those in the path of the storm.

2. Know thunderstorm facts:
    - Thunderstorms may occur singly, in clusters, or in lines.
    - Some of the most severe weather occurs when a single thunderstorm affects one location for an extended time.
    - Thunderstorms typically produce heavy rain for a brief period, anywhere from 30 minutes to an hour.
    - Warm, humid conditions are very favorable for thunderstorm development.
    - A typical thunderstorm is 15 miles in diameter and lasts an average of 30 minutes.
    - Of the estimated 100,000 thunderstorms each year in the United States, about 10 percent are classified as severe.
    - A thunderstorm is classified as severe if it produces hail at least three-quarters of an inch in diameter, has winds of 58 miles per hour or higher, or produces a tornado.

3. Know the calculation to determine how close you are to a thunderstorm:
    - Count the number of seconds between a flash of lightning and the next clap of thunder. Divide this number by 5 to determine the distance to the lightning in miles.

4. Remove dead or rotting trees and branches that could fall and cause injury or damage during a severe thunderstorm.

5. When a thunderstorm approaches, secure outdoor objects that could blow away or cause damage. Shutter windows, if possible, and secure outside doors. If shutters are not available, close window blinds, shades, or curtains.

Lightning

The ingredient that defines a thunderstorm is lightning. Since lightning creates thunder, a storm producing lightning is called a thunderstorm. Lightning occurs during all thunderstorms. Lightning results from the buildup and discharge of electrical energy between positively and negatively charged areas. The unpredictability of lightning increases the risk to individuals and property. On average, in the United States, 300 people are injured and 80 people are killed each year by lightning. Although most lightning victims survive, people struck by lightning often report a variety of long-term, debilitating symptoms, including memory loss, attention deficits, sleep disorders, numbness, dizziness, stiffness in joints, irritability, fatigue, weakness, muscle spasms, depression, and an inability to sit for a long period of time.

When thunderstorms threaten your area, get inside a home, building or hard-top automobile (not a convertible) and stay away from metallic objects and fixtures.
1. If you are inside a home:
    - Avoid showering or bathing. Plumbing and bathroom fixtures can conduct electricity.
    - Avoid using a corded telephone, except for emergencies. Cordless and cellular telephones are safe to use.
    - Unplug appliances and other electrical items, such as computers, and turn off air conditioners. Power surges from lightning can cause serious damage.
    - Use your battery-operated NOAA Weather Radio for updates from local officials.

2. If outside, with no time to reach a safe location, follow these recommendations:
    - In a forest, seek shelter in a low area under a thick growth of small trees.
        - In open areas, go to a low place, such as a ravine or valley. Be alert for flash floods.
        - Do not stand under a natural lightning rod, such as a tall, isolated tree in an open area.
        - Do not stand on a hilltop, in an open field, on the beach or in a boat on the water.
        - Avoid isolated sheds or other small structures in open areas.

- Get away from open water. If you are boating or swimming, get to land and find shelter immediately.
- Get away from anything metal – tractors, farm equipment, motorcycles, golf carts, golf clubs and bicycles.
- Stay away from wire fences, clotheslines, metal pipes, rails and other metallic paths that could carry lightning to you from some distance away.
- If you feel your hair stand on end (which indicates that lightning is about to strike), squat low to the ground on the balls of your feet. Place your hands over your ears and your head between your knees.

3. Make yourself the smallest target possible and minimize your contact with the ground. DO NOT lie flat on the ground.
4. Remember the following facts and safety tips about lightning.
Facts:
- Lightning often strikes outside of heavy rain and may occur as far as 10 miles away from any rainfall.
- Lightning-strike victims carry no electrical charge and should be attended to immediately. If breathing has stopped, begin mouth-to-mouth resuscitation. If the heart has stopped, a trained person should administer CPR. If the victim has a pulse and is breathing, look for other possible injuries. Check for burns where the lightning entered and left the body. Be alert also for nervous system damage, broken bones, and loss of hearing or eyesight. Contact your local emergency management office or American Red Cross chapter for information on CPR and first-aid classes.
- "Heat lightning" is actually lightning from a thunderstorm too far away for thunder to be heard. However, the storm may be moving in your direction!
- Most lightning deaths and injuries occur when people are caught outdoors in the summer months during the afternoon and evening.
- Lightning starts many fires in the western United States and Alaska.
- Lightning can occur from cloud-to-cloud, within a cloud, cloud-to-ground, or cloud-to-air.
- Your chances of being struck by lightning are estimated to be 1 in 600,000 but could be better by following safety tips.

Safety Tips:
- Postpone outdoor activities if thunderstorms are likely.

- Remember the 30/30 lightning safety rule – Go inside if, after seeing lighting, you cannot count to 30 before hearing thunder. Stay indoors for 30 minutes after hearing the last clap of thunder.
- Rubber-soled shoes and rubber tires provide NO protection from lightning. However, the steel frame of a hard-topped vehicle provides increased protection if you are not touching metal.

Although you may be injured if lightning strikes your car, you are much safer inside a vehicle than outside.

Tornadoes

Tornadoes are nature's most violent storms. Spawned from powerful thunderstorms, tornadoes can uproot trees, destroy buildings and turn harmless objects into deadly missiles. They can devastate a neighborhood in seconds. A tornado appears as a rotating, funnel-shaped cloud that extends to the ground with whirling winds that can reach 300 miles per hour. Damage paths can be in excess of one mile wide and 50 miles long. Every state is at some risk from this hazard.

Tornado Facts
1. A tornado is a violently rotating column of air extending from a thunderstorm to the ground.
2. Tornadoes are capable of destroying homes and vehicles and can cause fatalities.
3. Tornadoes may strike quickly, with little or no warning.
4. Tornadoes may appear nearly transparent until dust and debris are picked up or a cloud forms in the funnel. The average tornado moves SW to NE but tornadoes have been known to move in any direction.
5. The average forward speed is 30 mph but may vary from stationary to 70 mph with rotating winds that can reach 300 miles per hour.
6. Tornadoes can accompany tropical storms and hurricanes as they move onto land.
7. Waterspouts are tornadoes that form over water.
8. Tornadoes are most frequently reported east of the Rocky Mountains during spring and summer months, but can occur in any state at any time of year.
9. In the southern states, peak tornado season is March through May, while peak months in the northern states are during the late spring and early summer.

10. Tornadoes are most likely to occur between 3 p.m. and 9 p.m., but can occur at any time of the day or night.

What to do Before Tornadoes Threaten

1. Know the terms used to describe tornado threats:

Tornado Watch – Tornadoes are possible. Remain alert for approaching storms. Listen to your battery-operated NOAA Weather Radio or local radio/television outlets for updated reports.

Tornado Warning – A tornado has been sighted or indicated by weather radar. Take shelter immediately.

2. Ask your local emergency management office or American Red Cross chapter about the tornado threat in your area. Ask about community warning signals.

3. Purchase a NOAA Weather Radio with a battery backup and tone-alert feature that automatically alerts you when a Watch or Warning is issued (tone alert is not available in some areas). Purchase a battery-powered commercial radio and extra batteries as well.

4. Know the county or parish in which you live. Counties and parishes are used in Watches and Warnings to identify the location of tornadoes.

5. Determine places to seek shelter, such as a basement or storm cellar. If an underground shelter is not available, identify an interior room or hallway on the lowest floor.

6. Practice going to your shelter with your household.

7. Know the locations of designated shelters in places where you and your household spend time, such as public buildings, nursing homes and shopping centers. Ask local officials whether a registered engineer or architect has inspected your children's schools for shelter space.

8. Ask your local emergency manager or American Red Cross chapter if there are any public safe rooms or shelters nearby. See the "Safe Room and Shelter" section at the end of this chapter for more information.

9. Assemble a disaster supply kit. Keep a stock of food and extra drinking water. See the "Emergency Planning and Disaster Supplies" and "Evacuation" sections for more information.

10. Make a record of your personal property. Take photographs or videotapes of your belongings. Store these documents in a safe place.

What to do During a Tornado Watch

1. Listen to NOAA Weather Radio or to commercial radio or television newscasts for the latest information.

2. Be alert for approaching storms. If you see any revolving funnel-shaped clouds, report them immediately by telephone to your local police department or sheriff's office.
3. Watch for tornado danger signs:
- Dark, often greenish sky
- Large hail
- A large, dark, low-lying cloud (particularly if rotating)
- Loud roar, similar to a freight train

Caution:
- Some tornadoes are clearly visible, while rain or nearby low-hanging clouds obscure others.
- Occasionally, tornadoes develop so rapidly that little, if any, advance warning is possible.
- Before a tornado hits, the wind may die down and the air may become very still.
- A cloud of debris can mark the location of a tornado even if a funnel is not visible.
- Tornadoes generally occur near the trailing edge of a thunderstorm. It is not uncommon to see clear, sunlit skies behind a tornado.

4. Avoid places with wide-span roofs, such as auditoriums, cafeterias, large hallways, supermarkets or shopping malls.
5. Be prepared to take shelter immediately. Gather household members and pets. Assemble supplies to take to the shelter, such as flashlight, battery-powered radio, water and first-aid kit.

What to do During a Tornado Warning
When a tornado has been sighted, go to your shelter immediately.
1. In a residence or small building, move to a pre-designated shelter, such as a basement, storm cellar or "Safe Room or Shelter."
2. If there is no basement, go to an interior room on the lower level (closets, interior hallways). Put as many walls as possible between you and the outside. Get under a sturdy table and use arms to protect your head and neck. Stay there until the danger has passed.
3. Do not open windows. Use the time to seek shelter.
4. Stay away from windows, doors and outside walls. Go to the center of the room. Stay away from corners because they attract debris.
5. In a school, nursing home, hospital, factory or shopping center, go to predetermined shelter areas. Interior hallways on the lowest floor are usually safest. Stay away from windows and open spaces.

6. In a high-rise building, go to a small, interior room or hallway on the lowest floor possible.

7. Get out of vehicles, trailers and mobile homes immediately and go to the lowest floor of a sturdy nearby building or a storm shelter. Mobile homes, even if tied down, offer little protection from tornadoes.

8. If caught outside with no shelter, lie flat in a nearby ditch or depression and cover your head with your hands. Be aware of potential for flooding.

9. Do not get under an overpass or bridge. You are safer in a low, flat location.

10. Never try to outrun a tornado in urban or congested areas in a car or truck; instead, leave the vehicle immediately for safe shelter. Tornadoes are erratic and move swiftly.

11. Watch out for flying debris. Flying debris from tornadoes causes most fatalities and injuries.

What to do After a Tornado

1. Look out for broken glass and downed power lines.

2. Check for injuries. Do not attempt to move seriously injured people unless they are in immediate danger of death or further injury. If you must move an unconscious person, first stabilize the neck and back, and then call for help immediately.

- If the victim is not breathing, carefully position the victim for artificial respiration, clear the airway and commence mouth-to-mouth resuscitation.
- Maintain body temperature with blankets. Be sure the victim does not become overheated.
- Never try to feed liquids to an unconscious person.

3. Use caution when entering a damaged building. Be sure that walls, ceiling and roof are in place and that the structure rests firmly on the foundation. Wear sturdy work boots and gloves.

4. See the "Recovering From Disaster" section for more important information.

Wind "Safe Room and Shelter"

Extreme windstorms in many parts of the country pose a serious threat to buildings and their occupants. Your residence may be built "to code," but that does not mean that it can withstand winds from extreme events like tornadoes or major hurricanes.

The purpose of a wind shelter or "Safe Room" is to provide a space where you and your household can seek refuge that provides a high level of protection. You can build a shelter in one of the several places in your home:
- In your basement
- Beneath a concrete slab-on-grade foundation or garage floor
- In an interior room on the first floor

Shelters built below ground level provide the greatest protection, but a shelter built in a first-floor interior room can also provide the necessary protection. Below-ground shelters must be designed to avoid accumulating water during the heavy rains that often accompany severe windstorms.

To protect its occupants, an in-house shelter must be built to withstand high winds and flying debris, even if the rest of the residence is severely damaged or destroyed. Therefore:
- The shelter must be adequately anchored to resist overturning and uplift.
- The walls, ceiling, and door of the shelter must withstand wind pressure and resist penetration by windborne objects and falling debris.
- The connections between all parts of the shelter must be strong enough to resist the wind.
- If sections of either interior or exterior residence walls are used as walls of the shelter, they must be separated from the structure of the residence, so that damage to the residence will not cause damage to the shelter.

If you are concerned about wind hazards where you live, especially if you live in a high-risk area, you should consider building a shelter. Publications are available from FEMA to assist in determining if you need a shelter and how to construct one. Contact the FEMA distribution center for a copy of Taking Shelter from the Storm (L-233 for the brochure and FEMA-320 for the booklet with complete construction plans).

Winter Storms and Extreme Cold

Heavy snowfall and extreme cold can immobilize an entire region. Even areas that normally experience mild winters can be hit with a major snowstorm or extreme cold. The impacts include flooding, storm surge, closed highways, blocked roads, downed power lines and hypothermia. You can protect yourself and your household from the many hazards of winter by planning ahead.

What to do Before a Winter Storm Threatens
1. Know the terms used by weather forecasters:
    - Freezing rain – Rain that freezes when it hits the ground, creating a coating of ice on roads, walkways, trees and power lines
    - Sleet – Rain that turns to ice pellets before reaching the ground (Sleet also causes roads to freeze and become slippery.)
    - Winter Storm Watch – A winter storm is possible in your area
    - Winter Storm Warning – A winter storm is occurring, or will soon occur in your area
    - Blizzard Warning – Sustained winds or frequent gusts to 35 miles-per-hour or greater and considerable falling or blowing snow (reducing visibility to less than a quarter mile) are expected to prevail for a period of three hours or longer
    - Frost/Freeze Warning – Below-freezing temperatures are expected

2. Prepare to survive on your own for at least three days. Assemble a disaster supply kit. Be sure to include winter-specific items, such as rock salt to melt ice on walkways, sand to improve traction, snow shovels and other snow removal equipment. Keep a stock of food and extra drinking water. See the "Emergency Planning and Disaster Supplies" and "Evacuation" sections for more information. Prepare for possible isolation in your home:
    - Have sufficient heating fuel; regular fuel sources may be cut off.
    - Have emergency heating equipment and fuel (a gas fireplace or a wood-burning stove or fireplace) so you can keep at least one room of your residence livable. (Be sure the room is well ventilated.) If a thermostat controls your furnace and your electricity is cut off by a storm, you will need emergency heat.
    - Kerosene heaters are another emergency-heating option.
    - Store a good supply of dry, seasoned wood for your fireplace or wood-burning stove.
    - Keep fire extinguishers on hand, and make sure your household knows how to use them.
    - Never burn charcoal indoors.
3. Winterize your home to extend the life of your fuel supply:
    - Insulate walls and attics.
    - Caulk and weather-strip doors and windows.
    - Install storm windows or cover windows with plastic.

4. Maintain several days' supply of medicines, water, and food that needs no cooking or refrigeration.
5. What to do during a winter storm:
- Listen to the radio or television for weather reports and emergency information.
- Eat regularly and drink ample fluids, but avoid caffeine and alcohol.

6. Dress for the season:
- Wear several layers of loose fitting, lightweight and warm clothing rather than one layer of heavy clothing. The outer garments should be tightly woven and water repellent.
- Mittens are warmer than gloves.
- Wear a hat; most body heat is lost through the top of the head if the head is uncovered.
- Cover your mouth with a scarf to protect your lungs.

7. Be careful when shoveling snow. Over-exertion can bring on a heart attack – a major cause of death in the winter. If you must shovel snow, stretch before going outside and don't overexert yourself.

8. Watch for signs of frostbite: loss of feeling and white or pale appearance in extremities, such as fingers, toes, ear lobes or the tip of the nose. If symptoms are detected, get medical help immediately.

9. Watch for signs of hypothermia: uncontrollable shivering, memory loss, disorientation, incoherence, slurred speech, drowsiness and apparent exhaustion. If symptoms of hypothermia are detected, get the victim to a warm location, remove any wet clothing, warm the center of the body first, and give warm, non-alcoholic beverages if the victim is conscious. Get medical help as soon as possible.

10. When at home:
- Conserve fuel if necessary by keeping your residence cooler than normal. Temporarily "close off" heat to some rooms.
- When using kerosene heaters, maintain ventilation to avoid build-up of toxic fumes. Refuel kerosene heaters outside and keep them at least three feet from flammable objects.

Winter Driving

About 70 percent of winter deaths related to snow and ice occur in automobiles. Consider public transportation if you must travel. If you travel by car, travel in the day, don't travel alone, and keep others informed of your schedule. Stay on main roads; avoid back-road shortcuts.

1. Winterize your car. This includes a battery check, antifreeze, wipers and windshield-washer fluid, ignition system, thermostat, lights, flashing hazard

lights, exhaust system, heater, brakes, defroster, oil level, and tires. Consider snow tires, snow tires with studs, or chains. Keep your car's gas tank full.

2. Carry a "winter car kit" in the trunk of your car. The kit should include:
- Shovel
- Windshield scraper
- Battery-powered radio
- Flashlight
- Extra batteries
- Water
- Snack food
- Mittens
- Hat
- Blanket
- Tow chain or rope
- Tire chains
- Bag of road salt and sand
- Fluorescent distress flag
- Booster cables
- Roadmaps
- Emergency flares
- Cellular telephone or two-way radio, if available

3. If a blizzard traps you in your car:
- Pull off the highway. Turn on hazard lights and hang a distress flag from the radio aerial or window.
- Remain in your vehicle where rescuers are most likely to find you. Do not set out on foot unless you can see a building close by where you know you can take shelter. Be careful: distances are distorted by blowing snow. A building may seem close but be too far to walk to in deep snow.
- Run the engine and heater about 10 minutes each hour to keep warm. When the engine is running, open a window slightly for ventilation. This will protect you from possible carbon monoxide poisoning. Periodically clear snow from the exhaust pipe.
- Exercise to maintain body heat, but avoid overexertion. In extreme cold, use roadmaps, seat covers and floor mats for insulation. Huddle with passengers and use your coat for a blanket.
- Take turns sleeping. One person should be awake at all times to look for rescue crews.
- Drink fluids to avoid dehydration.

- Be careful not to waste battery power. Balance electrical energy needs – the use of lights, heat and radio – with supply.
- At night, turn on the inside light so work crews or rescuers can see you.
- If stranded in a remote area, spread a large cloth over the snow to attract attention of rescue personnel who may be surveying the area by airplane.
- Once the blizzard passes, you may need to leave the car and proceed on foot.

Extreme Heat

(Heat Wave)
Heat kills by pushing the human body beyond its limits. Under normal conditions, the body's internal thermostat produces perspiration that evaporates and cools the body. However, in extreme heat and high humidity, evaporation is slowed and the body must work extra hard to maintain a normal temperature. Most heat disorders occur because the victim has been overexposed to heat or has over-exercised for his or her age and physical condition. The elderly, young children and those who are sick or overweight are more likely to succumb to extreme heat.

Conditions that can induce heat-related illnesses include stagnant atmospheric conditions and poor air quality. Consequently, people living in urban areas may be at greater risk from the effects of a prolonged heat wave than those living in rural areas. Also, asphalt and concrete store heat longer and gradually release heat at night, which can produce higher nighttime temperatures known as the "urban heat island effect."

What to do Before an Extreme Heat Emergency
1. Know the terms associated with extreme heat:
    - Heat wave – Prolonged period of excessive heat, often combined with excessive humidity.
    - Heat index – A number in degrees Fahrenheit (F) that tells how hot it feels when relative humidity is added to the air temperature. Exposure to full sunshine can increase the heat index by 15 degrees.
    - Heat cramps – Muscular pains and spasms due to heavy exertion. Although heat cramps are the least severe, they are often the first signal that the body is having trouble with the heat.

- Heat exhaustion – Typically occurs when people exercise heavily or work in a hot, humid place where body fluids are lost through heavy sweating. Blood flow to the skin increases, causing blood flow to decrease to the vital organs. This results in a form of mild shock. If not treated, the victim's condition will worsen. Body temperature will keep rising and the victim may suffer heat stroke.
- Heat stroke – Heat stroke is life-threatening. The victim's temperature-control system, which produces sweating to cool the body, stops working. The body's temperature can increase so high that brain damage and death may result if the body is not cooled quickly.
- Sun stroke – Another term for heat stroke.

2. Consider the following preparedness measures when faced with the possibility of extreme heat:
    - Install window air conditioners snugly, insulate if necessary.
    - Close any floor heat registers nearby, and use a circulating or box fan to spread cool air.
    - Check air-conditioning ducts for proper insulation.
    - Install temporary reflectors, such as aluminum foil covered cardboard, to reflect heat back outside and be sure to weather-strip doors and sills to keep cool air in.
    - Cover windows that receive morning or afternoon sun with drapes, shades, awnings or louvers.
    - Outdoor awnings or louvers can reduce the heat that enters a home by up to 80 percent. Consider keeping storm windows up all year.

3. See the "Emergency Planning and Disaster Supplies" section for more information.

What to do During Extreme Heat or a Heat-wave Emergency

1. Stay indoors as much as possible:
    - If air conditioning is not available, stay on the lowest floor out of the sunshine.
    - Remember that electric fans do not cool; they just blow hot air around.

2. Eat well-balanced, light and regular meals. Avoid using salt tablets unless directed to do so by a physician.

3. Drink plenty of water regularly even if you do not feel thirsty:
    - People who have epilepsy or heart, kidney, or liver disease, are on fluid-restrictive diets, or have a problem with fluid retention should consult a doctor before increasing liquid intake.

4. Limit intake of alcoholic beverages:
    - Although beer and alcoholic beverages appear to satisfy thirst, they actually cause further body dehydration.
5. Never leave children or pets alone in closed vehicles.
6. Dress in loose clothes that cover as much skin as possible.
    - Lightweight, light-colored clothing reflects heat and sunlight and helps maintain normal body temperature.
7. Protect your face and head by wearing a wide-brimmed hat.
8. Avoid too much sunshine:
    - Sunburn slows the skin's ability to cool itself. Use a sunscreen lotion with a high SPF (sun protection factor) rating (i.e., 15 or greater).
9. Avoid strenuous work during the warmest part of the day. Use a buddy system when working in extreme heat and take frequent breaks.
10. Spend at least two hours per day in an air-conditioned place. If your home is not air conditioned, consider spending the warmest part of the day in public buildings, such as libraries, schools, movie theaters, shopping malls and other community facilities.
11. Check on family, friends and neighbors who do not have air conditioning and who spend much of their time alone.

First Aid for Heat-induced Illnesses
1. Sunburn
    - Symptoms: Skin redness and pain, possible swelling, blisters, fever, headaches.
    - First aid: Take a shower, using soap, to remove oils that may block pores, preventing the body from cooling naturally. If blisters occur, apply dry, sterile dressings and get medical attention.
2. Heat cramps
    - Symptoms: Painful spasms, usually in leg and abdominal muscles. Heavy sweating.
    - First aid: Get the victim to a cooler location. Lightly stretch and gently massage affected muscles to relieve spasm. Give sips of up to a half glass of cool water every 15 minutes. Do not give liquids with caffeine or alcohol. If nauseous, discontinue liquids.
3. Heat exhaustion
    - Symptoms: Heavy sweating and skin may be cool, pale or flushed. Weak pulse. Normal body temperature is possible but temperature will likely rise. Fainting or dizziness, nausea or vomiting, exhaustion and headaches are possible.

- First aid: Get victim to lie down in a cool place. Loosen or remove clothing. Apply cool, wet cloths. Fan or move victim to air-conditioned place. Give sips of water if victim is conscious. Be sure water is consumed slowly. Give half a glass of cool water every 15 minutes. If nausea occurs, discontinue. If vomiting occurs, seek immediate medical attention.

4. Heat stroke (sun stroke)
   - Symptoms: High body temperature (105+). Hot, red, dry skin. Rapid, weak pulse; and rapid, shallow breathing. Possible unconsciousness. Victim will likely not sweat unless victim was sweating from recent strenuous activity.
   - First aid: Heat stroke is a severe medical emergency. Call 911 or emergency medical services or get the victim to a hospital immediately. Delay can be fatal. Move victim to a cooler environment. Remove clothing. Try a cool bath, sponging or wet sheet to reduce body temperature. Watch for breathing problems. Use extreme caution. Use fans and air conditioners.

Emergency Water Shortage

A prolonged drought, poor water supply management, or contamination of a surface water supply source or aquifer can cause an emergency water shortage.

A drought is a period of abnormally dry weather that persists long enough to produce serious effects (crop damage, water supply shortages, etc.). The severity of the drought depends upon the degree of moisture deficiency, the duration, and the size of the affected area. Drought can affect vast territorial regions and large population numbers. In effect, drought is a silent but very damaging phenomenon that is rarely lethal but enormously destructive. Drought can ruin local and regional economies that are agricultural and tourism based. Drought also creates environmental conditions that increase risk of other hazards, such as fire, flash flood, and possible landslides/debris flow.

Poor water-quality management can result in the demand for water exceeding the available supply. This can be exacerbated by fluctuations in regional precipitation, excessive water demand, or rapid residential development.

Emergency water shortages can also be caused by contamination of a water supply. A major spill of a petroleum product or hazardous chemical on a major river can force communities to shut down water treatment plants. Although typically more localized, the contamination of ground water or an aquifer can also disrupt the use of well water.

Water Conservation
Conserving water is very important during emergency water shortages. Water saved by one user may be enough to protect the critical needs of others. Irrigation practices can be changed to use less water, and crops that use less water can be planted. Cities and towns can ration water, factories can change manufacturing methods, and individuals can practice water-saving measures to reduce consumption. If everyone reduces water use during a drought, more water will be available to share.

1. Practice indoor water conservation.

General:
- Never pour water down the drain when there may be another use for it. Use it to water your indoor plants or garden.
- Repair dripping faucets by replacing washers. One drop per second wastes 2,700 gallons of water per year!

Bathroom:
- Check all plumbing for leaks. Have leaks repaired by a plumber.
- Install a toilet displacement device to cut down on the amount of water needed to flush. Place a one-gallon plastic jug of water into the tank to displace toilet flow (do not use a brick, it may dissolve and loose pieces may cause damage to the internal parts). Be sure installation does not interfere with the operating parts.
- Consider purchasing a low-volume toilet that uses less than half the water of older models. NOTE: The law requires low-volume units in many areas.
- Replace your showerhead with an ultra-low-flow version.
- Do not take baths – take short showers – only turn on water to get wet and lather and then again to rinse off.
- Place a bucket in the shower to catch excess water for watering plants.
- Don't let the water run while brushing your teeth, washing your face or shaving.
- Don't flush the toilet unnecessarily. Dispose of tissues, insects, and other similar waste in the trash rather than the toilet.

Kitchen:
- Operate automatic dishwashers only when they are fully loaded. Use the "light wash" feature if available to use less water.
- Hand-wash dishes by filling two containers – one with soapy water and the other with rinse water containing a small amount of chlorine bleach.
- Most dishwashers can clean soiled dishes very well, so dishes do not have to be rinsed before washing. Just remove large particles of food, and put the soiled dishes in the dishwasher.
- Store drinking water in the refrigerator. Don't let the tap run while you are waiting for water to cool.
- Do not waste water waiting for it to get hot. Capture it for other uses, such as plant watering or heat it on the stove or in a microwave.
- Do not use running water to thaw meat or other frozen foods. Defrost food overnight in the refrigerator, or use the defrost setting on your microwave.
- Clean vegetables in a pan filled with water rather than running water from the tap.
- Kitchen sink disposals require a lot of water to operate properly. Start a compost pile as an alternate method of disposing of food waste, or simply dispose of food in the garbage.

Laundry:
- Operate automatic clothes washers only when they are fully loaded or set the water level for the size of your load.

Long-term indoor water conservation:
- Retrofit all household faucets by installing aerators with flow restrictors.
- Consider installing an instant hot water heater on your sink.
- Insulate your water pipes to reduce heat loss and prevent them from breaking if you have a sudden and unexpected spell of freezing weather.
- If you are considering installing a new heat pump or air-conditioning system, the new air-to-air models are just as efficient as the water-to-air type, and they do not waste water.
- Install a water-softening system only when the minerals in the water would damage your pipes. Turn the softener off while on vacation.
- When purchasing a new appliance, choose one that is more energy and water efficient.

2. Practice outdoor water conservation.

General:
- If you have a well at home, check your pump periodically. If the automatic pump turns on and off while water is not being used, you have a leak.

Car washing:
- Use a shut-off nozzle on your hose that can be adjusted down to a fine spray, so that water flows only as needed.
- Consider using a commercial car wash that recycles water. If you wash your own car, park on the grass so that you will be watering it at the same time.

Lawn-care:
- Don't over water your lawn. A heavy rain eliminates the need for watering for up to two weeks. Most of the year, lawns only need one inch of water per week.
- Water in several short sessions rather than one long one in order for your lawn to better absorb moisture.
- Position sprinklers so water lands on the lawn and shrubs and not on paved areas.
- Avoid sprinklers that spray a fine mist. Mist can evaporate before it reaches the lawn. Check sprinkler systems and timing devices regularly to be sure they operate properly.
- Raise the lawn-mower blade to at least three inches, or to its highest level. A higher cut encourages grass roots to grow deeper, shades the root system, and holds soil moisture.
- Plant drought-resistant lawn seed.
- Avoid over-fertilizing your lawn. Applying fertilizer increases the need for water. Apply fertilizers that contain slow-release, water-insoluble forms of nitrogen.
- Use a broom or blower instead of a hose to clean leaves and other debris from your driveway or sidewalk.
- Do not leave sprinklers or hoses unattended. A garden hose can pour out 600 gallons or more in only a few hours.

Pool:
- Consider installing a new water-saving pool filter. A single back flushing with a traditional filter uses 180 to 250 gallons of water.
- Cover pools and spas to reduce evaporation of water.

Long-term outdoor conservation:
- Plant native and/or drought-tolerant grasses, ground covers, shrubs and trees. Once established, they do not need water as frequently and usually will survive a dry period without watering. Small plants

require less water to become established. Group plants together based on similar water needs.
- Install irrigation devices that are the most water efficient for each use. Micro and drip irrigation and soaker hoses are examples of efficient devices.
- Use mulch to retain moisture in the soil. Mulch also helps control weeds that compete with landscape plants for water.
- Avoid purchasing recreational water toys that require a constant stream of water.
- Avoid installing ornamental water features (such as fountains) unless they use recycled water.

Participate in public water-conservation programs of your local government, utility or water management district. Follow water conservation and water shortage rules in effect. Remember, you are included in the restrictions even if your water comes from a private well. Be sure to support community efforts that help develop and promote a water-conservation ethic. Contact your local water authority, utility district, or local emergency management agency for information specific to your area.

Earthquakes

An earthquake is a sudden shaking of the earth caused by the breaking and shifting of rock beneath the earth's surface. Earthquakes can cause buildings and bridges to collapse, telephone and power lines to fall, and result in fires, explosions and landslides. Earthquakes can also cause huge ocean waves, called tsunamis, which travel long distances over water until they crash into coastal areas.

The following information includes general guidelines for earthquake preparedness and safety. Because injury-prevention techniques may vary from state to state, it is recommended that you contact your local emergency management office, health department, or American Red Cross chapter.

What to do Before an Earthquake
1. Know the terms associated with earthquakes.
Earthquake – a sudden slipping or movement of a portion of the earth's crust accompanied and followed by a series of vibrations.

Aftershock – an earthquake of similar or lesser intensity that follows the main earthquake.

Fault – the earth's crust slips along a fault, an area of weakness where two sections of crust have separated. The crust may only move a few inches to a few feet in a severe earthquake.

Epicenter – the area of the earth's surface directly above the origin of an earthquake.

Seismic Waves – vibrations that travel outward from the center of the earthquake at speeds of several miles per second. These vibrations can shake some buildings so rapidly that they collapse.

Magnitude – indicates how much energy was released. This energy can be measured on a recording device and graphically displayed through lines on a Richter Scale. A magnitude of 7.0 on the Richter Scale would indicate a very strong earthquake. Each whole number on the scale represents an increase of about 30 times the energy released. Therefore, an earthquake measuring 6.0 is about 30 times more powerful than one measuring 5.0.

2. Look for items in your home that could become a hazard in an earthquake:
- Repair defective electrical wiring, leaky gas lines, and inflexible utility connections.
- Bolt down water heaters and gas appliances (have an automatic gas shut-off device installed that is triggered by an earthquake).
- Place large or heavy objects on lower shelves. Fasten shelves to walls. Brace high and top-heavy objects.
- Store bottled foods, glass, china and other breakables on low shelves or in cabinets that can fasten shut.
- Anchor overhead lighting fixtures.
- Check and repair deep plaster cracks in ceilings and foundations. Get expert advice, especially if there are signs of structural defects.
- Be sure the residence is firmly anchored to its foundation.
- Install flexible-pipe fittings to avoid gas or water leaks. Flexible fittings are more resistant to breakage.

3. Know where and how to shut off electricity, gas and water at main switches and valves. Check with your local utilities for instructions.

4. Hold earthquake drills with your household:
- Locate safe spots in each room under a sturdy table or against an inside wall. Reinforce this information by physically placing yourself and your household in these locations.

- Identify danger zones in each room – near windows where glass can shatter, bookcases or furniture that can fall over, or under ceiling fixtures that could fall down.

5. Develop a plan for reuniting your household after an earthquake. Establish an out-of-town telephone contact for household members to call to let others know that they are OK.

6. Review your insurance policies. Some damage may be covered even without specific earthquake insurance. Protect important home and business papers.

7. Prepare to survive on your own for at least three days. Assemble a disaster supply kit. Keep a stock of food and extra drinking water. See the "Emergency Planning and Disaster Supplies" and "Evacuation" sections for more information.

What to do During an Earthquake

Stay inside until the shaking stops and it is safe to go outside. Most injuries during earthquakes occur when falling objects hit people as they enter or exit buildings.

1. Drop, Cover and Hold On! Minimize your movements during an earthquake to a few steps to a nearby safe place. Stay indoors until the shaking has stopped and you are sure exiting is safe.

2. If you are indoors, take cover under a sturdy desk, table or bench, or against an inside wall, and hold on. Stay away from glass, windows, outside doors or walls and anything that could fall, such as lighting fixtures or furniture. If you are in bed, stay there, hold on and protect your head with a pillow, unless you are under a heavy light fixture that could fall.

3. If there isn't a table or desk near you, cover your face and head with your arms and crouch in an inside corner of the building. Doorways should only be used for shelter if they are in close proximity to you and if you know that they have a strongly supported load-bearing doorway.

4. If you are outdoors, stay there. Move away from buildings, streetlights and utility wires.

5. If you live in an apartment building or other multi-household structure with many levels, consider the following:
- Get under a desk and stay away from windows and outside walls.
- Stay in the building (many injuries occur as people flee a building and are struck by falling debris from above).
- Be aware that the electricity may go out and sprinkler systems may come on.
- DO NOT use the elevators.

6. If you are in a crowded indoor public location:
   - Stay where you are. Do not rush for the doorways.
   - Move away from tall shelves, cabinets and bookcases containing objects that may fall.
   - Take cover and grab something to shield your head and face from falling debris and glass.
   - Be aware that the electricity may go out or the sprinkler systems or fire alarms may turn on.
   - DO NOT use elevators.

7. In a moving vehicle, stop as quickly as safety permits, and stay in the vehicle. Avoid stopping near or under buildings, trees, overpasses or utility wires. Then, proceed cautiously, watching for road and bridge damage.

8. If you become trapped in debris:
   - Do not light a match.
   - Do not move about or kick up dust.
   - Cover your mouth with a handkerchief or clothing.
   - Tap on a pipe or wall so rescuers can locate you. Use a whistle if one is available. Shout only as a last resort – shouting can cause you to inhale dangerous amounts of dust.

9. Stay indoors until the shaking has stopped and you are sure exiting is safe.

What to do After an Earthquake

1. Be prepared for aftershocks. These secondary shock waves are usually less violent than the main quake but can be strong enough to do additional damage to weakened structures.

2. Check for injuries. Do not attempt to move seriously injured people unless they are in immediate danger of death or further injury. If you must move an unconscious person, first stabilize the neck and back, and then call for help immediately.
   - If the victim is not breathing, carefully position the victim for artificial respiration, clear the airway and start mouth-to-mouth resuscitation.
   - Maintain body temperature with blankets. Be sure the victim does not become overheated.
   - Never try to feed liquids to an unconscious person.

3. If the electricity goes out, use flashlights or battery powered lanterns. Do not use candles, matches or open flames indoors after the earthquake because of possible gas leaks.

4. In areas covered with fallen debris and broken glass, wear sturdy shoes.

5. Check your home for structural damage. If you have any doubts about safety, have your home inspected by a professional before entering.

6. Check chimneys for visual damage; however, have a professional inspect the chimney for internal damage before lighting a fire.

7. Clean up spilled medicines, bleaches, gasoline and other flammable liquids. Evacuate the building if gasoline fumes are detected and the building is not well ventilated.

8. Visually inspect utility lines and appliances for damage.
- If you smell gas or hear a hissing or blowing sound, open a window and leave. Shut off the main gas valve. Report the leak to the gas company from the nearest working phone or cell phone available.
- Stay out of the building. If you shut off the gas supply at the main valve, you will need a professional to turn it back on.
- Switch off electrical power at the main fuse box or circuit breaker if electrical damage is suspected or known.
- Shut off the water supply at the main valve if water pipes are damaged.
- Do not flush toilets until you know that sewage lines are intact.

9. Open cabinets cautiously. Beware of objects that can fall off shelves.

10. Use the phone only to report life-threatening emergencies.

11. Listen to news reports for the latest emergency information.

12. Stay off the streets. If you must go out, watch for fallen objects, downed electrical wires, weakened walls, bridges, roads and sidewalks.

13. Stay away from damaged areas unless your assistance has been specifically requested by police, fire or relief organizations.

14. If you live in coastal areas, be aware of possible tsunamis, sometimes mistakenly called tidal waves. When local authorities issue a tsunami warning, assume that a series of dangerous waves is on the way. Stay away from the beach. See the "Tsunamis" section for more information.

Volcanoes

A volcano is a vent through which molten rock escapes to the earth's surface. When pressure from gases within the molten rock becomes too great, an eruption occurs. Some eruptions are relatively quiet, producing lava flows that creep across the land at two to 10 miles per hour.

Explosive eruptions can shoot columns of gases and rock fragments tens of miles into the atmosphere, spreading ash hundreds of miles downwind. Lateral blasts can flatten trees for miles. Hot, sometimes poisonous, gases may flow down the sides of the volcano.

Lava flows are streams of molten rock that either pour from a vent quietly through lava tubes or by lava fountains. Because of their intense heat, lava flows are also great fire hazards. Lava flows destroy everything in their path, but most move slowly enough that people can move out of the way.

Fresh volcanic ash, made of pulverized rock, can be harsh, acidic, gritty, glassy and odorous. While not immediately dangerous to most adults, the combination of acidic gas and ash could cause lung damage to small infants, very old people or those suffering from severe respiratory illnesses. Volcanic ash can also damage machinery, including engines and electrical equipment. Ash accumulations mixed with water become heavy and can collapse roofs.

Volcanic eruptions can be accompanied by other natural hazards: earthquakes, mudflows and flash floods, rock falls and landslides, acid rain, fire, and (under special conditions) tsunamis. Active volcanoes in the U.S. are found mainly in Hawaii, Alaska and the Pacific Northwest.

What to do Before an Eruption
1. Make evacuation plans. If you live in a known volcanic hazard area, plan a route out and have a backup route in mind.
2. Develop a household disaster plan. In case household members are separated from one another during a volcanic eruption (a real possibility during the day when adults are at work and children are at school), have a plan for getting back together. Ask an out-of-town relative or friend to serve as the "household contact" because, after a disaster, it's often easier to call long distance. Make sure everyone knows the name, address, and phone number of the contact person.
3. Assemble a disaster supply kit (see "Emergency Planning and Disaster Supplies" section).
4. Get a pair of goggles and a throwaway breathing mask for each member of the household in case of ash-fall.
5. Do not visit an active volcano site unless officials designate a safe-viewing area.

What to do During an Eruption
1. If close to the volcano, evacuate immediately away from the volcano to avoid flying debris, hot gases, lateral blast and lava flow.
2. Avoid areas downwind from the volcano to avoid volcanic ash.
3. Be aware of mudflows. The danger from a mudflow increases as you approach a stream channel and decreases as you move away from a stream

channel toward higher ground. In some parts of the world (Central and South America, Indonesia, the Philippines), this danger also increases with prolonged heavy rains. Mudflows can move faster than you can walk or run. Look upstream before crossing a bridge, and do not cross if the mudflow is approaching. Avoid river valleys and low-lying areas.

4. Stay indoors until the ash has settled unless there is danger of the roof collapsing.

5. During an ash fall, close doors, windows, and all ventilation in the house (chimney vents, furnaces, air conditioners, fans and other vents).

6. Avoid driving in heavy dust unless absolutely required. If you do drive in dense dust, keep speed down to 35 mph or slower.

7. Remove heavy ash from flat or low-pitched roofs and rain gutters.

8. Volcanic ash is actually fine, glassy fragments and particles that can cause severe injury to breathing passages, eyes, and open wounds, and irritation to skin. Follow these precautions to keep yourself safe from ash-fall:
- Wear long-sleeved shirts and long pants.
- Use goggles and wear eyeglasses instead of contact lenses.
- Use a dust mask or hold a damp cloth over your face to help breathing.
- Keep car or truck engines off. Driving can stir up volcanic ash that can clog engines and stall vehicles. Moving parts can be damaged from abrasion, including bearings, brakes and transmissions.

What to do After the Eruption

1. Avoid ash-fall areas if possible. If you are in an ash-fall area, cover your mouth and nose with a mask, keep skin covered and wear goggles to protect the eyes.

2. Clear roofs of ash-fall because it is very heavy and can cause buildings to collapse. Exercise great caution when working on a roof.

3. Avoid driving through ash-fall that is easily stirred up and can clog engines, causing vehicles to stall.

4. If you have a respiratory ailment, avoid contact with any amount of ash. Stay indoors until local health officials advise it is safe to go outside.

Landslides and Debris Flow

(Mudslide)
Landslides occur in all U.S. states and territories and occur when masses of rock, earth, or debris move down a slope. Landslides may be small or large, and can move at slow or very high speeds. They are activated by storms,

earthquakes, volcanic eruptions, fires and by human modification of the land.

Debris and mudflows are rivers of rock, earth, and other debris saturated with water. They develop when water rapidly accumulates in the ground, during heavy rainfall or rapid snowmelt, changing the earth into a flowing river of mud or "slurry." They can flow rapidly down slopes or through channels, and can strike with little or no warning at avalanche speeds. They can also travel several miles from their source, growing in size as they pick up trees, large boulders, cars, and other materials along the way.

Landslide, mudflow, and debris-flow problems are occasionally caused by land mismanagement. Improper land-use practices on ground of questionable stability, particularly in mountain, canyon and coastal regions, can create and accelerate serious landslide problems. Land-use zoning, professional inspections, and proper design can minimize many landslide, mudflow, and debris-flow problems.

What to do Before a Landslide or Debris Flow
1. Contact your local emergency management office or American Red Cross chapter for information on local landslide and debris flow hazards.
2. Get a ground assessment of your property:
   - County or state geological experts, local planning department or departments of natural resources may have specific information on areas vulnerable to landslides. Consult an appropriate professional expert for advice on corrective measures you can take.
3. Minimize home hazards by having flexible-pipe fittings installed to avoid gas or water leaks. Flexible fittings are more resistant to breakage. Only the gas company or its professionals should install gas fittings.
4. Familiarize yourself with your surrounding area:
   - Small changes in your local landscape could alert you to the potential of greater future threat.
   - Observe the patterns of storm-water drainage on slopes and especially the places where runoff water converges.
   - Watch for any sign of land movement, such as small slides, flows, or progressively leaning trees, on the hillsides near your home.
5. Be particularly observant of your surrounding area before and during intense storms that could heighten the possibility of landslide or debris flow from heavy rains. Many debris-flow fatalities occur when people are sleeping.

6. Talk to your insurance agent. Debris flow may be covered by flood insurance policies from the National Flood Insurance Program (NFIP).
7. Learn to recognize landslide-warning signs.
- Doors or windows stick or jam for the first time.
- New cracks appear in plaster, tile, brick or foundations.
- Outside walls, walks or stairs begin pulling away from the building.
- Slowly developing, widening cracks appear on the ground or on paved areas, such as streets or driveways.
- Underground utility lines break.
- Bulging ground appears at the base of a slope.
- Water breaks through the ground surface in new locations.
- Fences, retaining walls, utility poles or trees tilt or move.
- You hear a faint rumbling sound that increases in volume as the landslide nears.
- The ground slopes downward in one specific direction and may begin shifting in that direction under your feet.

What to do During a Heightened Threat (intense storm) of Landslide or Debris Flow

1. Listen to radio or television for warnings of intense rainfall:
   - Be prepared to evacuate if instructed by local authorities or if you feel threatened.
   - Should you remain at home, move to a second story if possible to distance yourself from the direct path of debris flow and landslide debris.
2. Be alert when intense, short bursts of rain follow prolonged heavy rains or damp weather, which increases the risk of debris flows.
3. Listen for any unusual sounds that might indicate moving debris, such as trees cracking or boulders knocking together. A trickle of flowing or falling mud or debris may precede larger landslides. Moving debris can flow quickly and sometimes without warning.
4. If you are near a stream or channel, be alert for sudden increases or decreases in water flow and for a change from clear to muddy water. Such changes may indicate landslide activity upstream. Be prepared to move quickly.
5. Be especially alert when driving. Embankments along roadsides are particularly susceptible to landslides. Watch for collapsed pavement, mud, fallen rocks, and other indications of possible debris flows.
6. Evacuate when ordered by local authorities. See the "Evacuation" section for more information.

What to do During a Landslide or Debris Flow
1. Quickly move away from the path of a landslide or debris flow.
2. Areas generally considered safe include:
    - Areas that have not moved in the past.
    - Relatively flat-lying areas away from drastic changes in slope.
    - Areas at the top of or along ridges set back from the tops of slopes.
3. If escape is not possible, curl into a tight ball and protect your head.

What to do After a Landslide or Debris Flow
1. Stay away from the slide area. There may be danger of additional slides.
2. Check for injured and trapped people near the slide, without entering the direct slide area, and direct rescuers to them.
3. Help a neighbor who may require special assistance – large families, children, elderly people and people with disabilities.
4. Listen to local radio or television stations for the latest emergency information.
5. Landslides and flows can provoke associated dangers, such as broken electrical, water, gas and sewage lines, and disrupt roadways and railways:
    - Look for and report broken utility lines to appropriate authorities. Reporting potential hazards will get the utilities turned off as quickly as possible, preventing further hazard and injury.
    - Check the building foundation, chimney, and surrounding land for damage. Damage to foundations, chimneys, or surrounding land may help you assess the safety of the area.
6. Watch for flooding, which may occur after a landslide or debris flow. Floods sometimes follow landslides and debris flows because they may both be started by the same event.
7. Replant damaged ground as soon as possible since erosion caused by loss of ground cover can lead to flash flooding and additional landslides in the near future.
8. Seek the advice of a geotechnical expert for evaluating landslide hazards or designing corrective techniques to reduce landslide risk. A professional will be able to advise you of the best ways to prevent or reduce landslide risk, without creating further hazard.
9. See the "Recovering From Disaster" section for more information.

Tsunamis

Tsunami (pronounced sue-na-me), sometimes mistakenly called a tidal wave, is a series of enormous waves created by an underwater disturbance, such as an earthquake. A tsunami can move hundreds of miles per hour in the open ocean and smash into land with waves as high as 100 feet or more, although most waves are less than 18 feet high.

From the area where the tsunami originates, waves travel outward in all directions much like the ripples caused by throwing a rock into a pond. In deep water, the tsunami wave is not noticeable. Once the wave approaches the shore it builds in height. All tsunamis are potentially dangerous, even though they may not damage every coastline they strike. A tsunami can strike anywhere along most of the U.S. coastline. The most destructive tsunamis have occurred along the coasts of California, Oregon, Washington, Alaska and Hawaii.

Earthquake-induced movement of the ocean floor most often generates tsunamis. Landslides, volcanic eruptions, and even meteorites can also generate tsunamis. If a major earthquake or landslide occurs close to shore, the first wave in a series could reach the beach in a few minutes, even before a warning is issued.

Areas are at greater risk if less than 25 feet above sea level and within a mile of the shoreline. Drowning is the most common cause of death associated with a tsunami. Tsunami waves and the receding water are very destructive to structures in the run-up zone. Other hazards include flooding, contamination of drinking water and fires from gas lines or ruptured tanks.

What to do Before a Tsunami
 1. Know the terms used by the West Coast/Alaska Tsunami Warning Center (WC/ATWC – responsible for tsunami warnings for California, Oregon, Washington, British Columbia, and Alaska) and the Pacific Tsunami Warning Center (PTWC – responsible for tsunami warnings to international authorities, Hawaii, and the U.S. territories within the Pacific basin).
Advisory – An earthquake has occurred in the Pacific basin, which might generate a tsunami.
WC/ATWC and PTWC will issue hourly bulletins advising of the situation.
Watch – A tsunami was or may have been generated, but is at least two hours travel time to the area in Watch status.
Warning – A tsunami was or may have been generated, which could cause damage; therefore, people in the warning area are strongly advised to evacuate.
 2. Listen to radio or television for more information and follow the instructions of your local authorities.

3. Immediate warning of tsunamis sometimes comes in the form of a noticeable recession in water away from the shoreline. This is nature's tsunami warning, and it should be heeded by moving inland to higher ground immediately.

4. If you feel an earthquake in a coastal area, turn on your radio to learn if there is a tsunami warning.

5. Know that a small tsunami at one beach can be a giant wave a few miles away. The topography of the coastline and the ocean floor will influence the size of the wave.

6. A tsunami may generate more than one wave. Do not let the modest size of one wave allow you to forget how dangerous a tsunami is. The next wave may be bigger.

7. Prepare for possible evacuation. Learn evacuation routes. Determine where you would go and how you would get there if you needed to evacuate. See the "Evacuation" and "Emergency Planning and Disaster Supplies" sections for more information.

What to do During a Tsunami
1. If you are advised to evacuate, do so immediately.
2. Stay away from the area until local authorities say it is safe. Do not be fooled into thinking that the danger is over after a single wave – a tsunami is not a single wave but a series of waves that can vary in size.
3. Do not go to the shoreline to watch for a tsunami. When you can see the wave, it is too late to escape.

What to do After a Tsunami
1. Avoid flooded and damaged areas until officials say it is safe to return.
2. Stay away from debris in the water; it may pose a safety hazard to boats and people.
3. See the "Recovering From Disaster" section for more information.

Fire

Each year more than 4,000 Americans die and more than 25,000 are injured in fires, many of which could be prevented. Direct property loss due to fires is estimated at $8.6 billion annually.

To protect yourself, it's important to understand the basic characteristics of fire. Fire spreads quickly. There is no time to gather valuables or make a phone call. In just two minutes a fire can become life threatening. In five minutes a residence can be engulfed in flames.

Heat and smoke from fire can be more dangerous than the flames. Inhaling the super-hot air can sear your lungs. Fire produces poisonous gases that make you disoriented and drowsy. Instead of being awakened by a fire, you may fall into a deeper sleep. Asphyxiation is the leading cause of fire deaths, exceeding burns by a three-to-one ratio.

What to do Before Fire Strikes

1. Install smoke alarms. Working smoke alarms decrease your chances of dying in a fire by half:
    - Place smoke alarms on every level of your residence – outside bedrooms on the ceiling or high on the wall, at the top of open stairways or at the bottom of enclosed stairs and near (but not in) the kitchen.
    - Test and clean smoke alarms once a month and replace batteries at least once a year. Replace smoke alarms once every 10 years.

2. With your household, plan two escape routes from every room in the residence. Practice with your household escaping from each room:
    - Make sure windows are not nailed or painted shut. Make sure security gratings on windows have a fire safety-opening feature so that they can be easily opened from the inside.
    - Consider escape ladders if your home has more than one level and ensure that burglar bars and other anti-theft mechanisms that block outside window entry are easily opened from inside.
    - Teach household members to stay low to the floor (where the air is safer in a fire) when escaping from a fire.
    - Pick a place outside your home for the household to meet after escaping from a fire.

3. Clean out storage areas. Don't let trash, such as old newspapers and magazines, to accumulate.

4. Check the electrical wiring in your home:
    - Inspect extension cords for frayed or exposed wires or loose plugs.
    - Outlets should have cover plates and no exposed wiring.
    - Make sure wiring does not run under rugs, over nails, or across high-traffic areas.
    - Do not overload extension cords or outlets. If you need to plug in two or three appliances, get a UL-approved unit with built-in circuit breakers to prevent sparks and short circuits.
    - Make sure home insulation does not touch electrical wiring.
    - Have an electrician check the electrical wiring in your home.

5. Never use gasoline, benzine, naptha or similar liquids indoors:

- Store flammable liquids in approved containers in well-ventilated storage areas.
- Never smoke near flammable liquids.
- After use, safely discard all rags or materials soaked in flammable material.

6. Check heating sources. Many home fires are started by faulty furnaces or stoves, cracked or rusted furnace parts and chimneys with creosote build-up. Have chimneys, wood stoves and all home-heating systems inspected and cleaned annually by a certified specialist.

7. Insulate chimneys and place spark arresters on top. The chimney should be at least three feet higher than the roof. Remove branches hanging above and around the chimney.

8. Take care when using alternative heating sources, such as wood, coal and kerosene heaters and electrical space heaters:
- Check with your local fire department on the legality of using kerosene heaters in your community. Be sure to fill kerosene heaters outside after they have cooled.
- Place heaters at least three feet away from flammable materials. Make sure the floor and nearby walls are properly insulated.
- Use only the type of fuel designated for your unit and follow manufacturer's instructions.
- Store ashes in a metal container outside and away from the residence.
- Keep open flames away from walls, furniture, drapery and flammable items. Keep a screen in front of the fireplace.
- Have chimneys and wood stoves inspected annually and cleaned, if necessary.
- Use portable heaters only in well-ventilated rooms.

9. Keep matches and lighters up high, away from children, and if possible, in a locked cabinet.

10. Do not smoke in bed, or when drowsy or medicated. Provide smokers with deep, sturdy ashtrays. Douse cigarette and cigar butts with water before disposal.

11. Safety experts recommend that you sleep with your door closed.

12. Know the locations of the gas valve and electric fuse or circuit-breaker box and how to turn them off in an emergency. If you shut off your main gas line for any reason, allow only a gas company representative to turn it on again.

13. Install A-B-C type fire extinguishers in the home and teach household members how to use them (Type A – wood or papers fires only; Type B –

flammable liquid or grease fires; Type C – electrical fires; Type A-B-C – rated for all fires and recommended for the home).
14. Consider installing an automatic fire sprinkler system in your home.
15. Ask your local fire department to inspect your residence for fire safety and prevention.
16. Teach children how to report a fire and when to use 911.
17. To support insurance claims in case you do have a fire, conduct an inventory of your property and possessions and keep the list in a separate location. Photographs are also helpful.
18. See the "Emergency Planning and Disaster Supplies" section for additional information.

What to do During a Fire
1. Use water or a fire extinguisher to put out small fires. Do not try to put out a fire that is getting out of control. If you're not sure if you can control it, get everyone out of the residence and call the fire department from a neighbor's residence.
2. Never use water on an electrical fire. Use only a fire extinguisher approved for electrical fires.
3. Smother oil and grease fires in the kitchen with baking soda or salt, or put a lid over the flame if it is burning in a pan. Do not attempt to take the pan outside.
4. If your clothes catch fire, stop, drop and roll until the fire is extinguished. Running only makes the fire burn faster.
5. If you are escaping through a closed door, use the back of your hand to feel the top of the door, the doorknob, and the crack between the door and doorframe before you open it. Never use the palm of your hand or fingers to test for heat – burning those areas could impair your ability to escape a fire (i.e., ladders and crawling):
    - If the door is cool, open slowly and ensure fire and/or smoke is not blocking your escape route. If your escape route is blocked, shut the door immediately and use an alternate escape route, such as a window. If clear, leave immediately through the door. Be prepared to crawl. Smoke and heat rise. The air is clearer and cooler near the floor.
    - If the door is warm or hot, do not open. Escape through a window. If you cannot escape, hang a white or light-colored sheet outside the window, alerting fire fighters to your presence.
6. If you must exit through smoke, crawl low under the smoke to your exit – heavy smoke and poisonous gases collect first along the ceiling.

7. Close doors behind you as you escape to delay the spread of the fire.
8. Once you are safely out, stay out and call 911.

What to do After a Fire
1. Give first aid where needed. After calling 911 or your local emergency number, cool and cover burns to reduce chance of further injury or infection.
2. Do not enter a fire-damaged building unless authorities say it is OK.
3. If you must enter a fire-damaged building, be alert for heat and smoke. If you detect either, evacuate immediately.
4. Have an electrician check your household wiring before the current is turned on.
5. Do not attempt to reconnect any utilities yourself. Leave this to the fire department and other authorities.
6. Beware of structural damage. Roofs and floors may be weakened and need repair.
7. Contact your local disaster relief service, such as the American Red Cross or Salvation Army, if you need housing, food or a place to stay.
8. Call your insurance agent:
    - Make a list of damage and losses. Pictures are helpful.
    - Keep records of cleanup and repair costs. Receipts are important for both insurance and income tax claims.
    - Do not throw away any damaged goods until an official inventory has been taken. Your insurance company takes all damages into consideration.
9. If you are a tenant, contact the landlord. It's the property owner's responsibility to prevent further loss or damage to the site.
10. Secure personal belongings or move them to another location.
11. Discard food, beverages and medicines that have been exposed to heat, smoke or soot. Refrigerators and freezers left closed hold their temperature for a short time. Do not attempt to refreeze food that has thawed.
12. If you have a safe or strong box, do not try to open it. It can hold intense heat for several hours. If the door is opened before the box has cooled, the contents could burst into flames.
13. If a building inspector says the building is unsafe and you must leave your home:
    - Ask local police to watch the property during your absence.
    - Pack identification, medicines, glasses, jewelry, credit cards, checkbooks, insurance policies and financial records, if you can reach them safely.

- Notify friends, relatives, police and fire departments, your insurance agent, the mortgage company, utility companies, delivery services, employers, schools and the Post Office of your whereabouts.

14. See the "Shelter" and "Recovering From Disaster" sections for more information.

Wildland Fires

If you live on a remote hillside, in a valley, prairie or forest where flammable vegetation is abundant, your residence could be vulnerable to wildland fire. These fires are usually triggered by lightning or accidents.

1. Fire facts about rural living:
   - Once a fire starts outdoors in a rural area, it is often hard to control. Firefighters dealing with such fires are trained to protect natural resources, not homes and buildings.
   - Many homes are located far from fire stations. The result is longer emergency response times. Within a matter of minutes, an entire home may be destroyed by fire.
   - Limited water supply in rural areas can make fire suppression difficult.
   - Homes may be secluded and surrounded by woods, dense brush and combustible vegetation that fuel fires.

2. Ask fire authorities for information about wildland fires in your area. Request that they inspect your residence and property for hazards.

3. Be prepared and have a fire safety and evacuation plan:
   - Practice fire escape and evacuation plans.
   - Mark the entrance to your property with address signs that are clearly visible from the road.
   - Know which local emergency services are available and have those numbers posted near telephones.
   - Provide emergency-vehicle access through roads and driveways at least 12 feet wide with adequate turnaround space.

4. Tips for making your property fire resistant:
   - Keep lawns trimmed, leaves raked, and the roof and rain-gutters free from debris, such as dead limbs and leaves.
   - Stack firewood at least 30 feet away from your home.
   - Store flammable materials, liquids and solvents in metal containers outside the home, at least 30 feet away from structures and wooden fences.

- Create defensible space by thinning trees and brush within 30 feet around your home. Beyond 30 feet, remove dead wood, debris and low tree branches.
- Landscape your property with fire-resistant plants and vegetation to prevent fire from spreading quickly. For example, hardwood trees are more fire resistant than pine, evergreen, eucalyptus or fir trees.
- Make sure water sources, such as hydrants, ponds, swimming pools and wells, are accessible to the fire department.

5. Protect your home:
   - Use fire resistant, protective roofing and materials like stone, brick and metal to protect your home. Avoid using wood materials. They offer the least fire protection.
   - Cover all exterior vents, attics and eaves with metal mesh screens no larger than six millimeters or 1/4 inch to prevent debris from collecting and to help keep sparks out.
   - Install multi-pane windows, tempered safety glass or fireproof shutters to protect large windows from radiant heat.
   - Use fire-resistant draperies for added window protection.
   - Have chimneys, wood stoves and all home-heating systems inspected and cleaned annually by a certified specialist.
   - Insulate chimneys, and place spark arresters on top. Chimney should be at least three feet above the roof.
   - Remove branches hanging above and around the chimney.

6. Follow local burning laws:
   - Do not burn trash or other debris without proper knowledge of local burning laws, techniques and the safest times of day and year to burn.
   - Before burning debris in a wooded area, make sure you notify local authorities and obtain a burning permit.
   - Use an approved incinerator with a safety lid or covering with holes no larger than 3/4 inch.
   - Create at least a 10-foot clearing around the incinerator before burning debris.
   - Have a fire extinguisher or garden hose on hand when burning debris.

7. If wildfire threatens your home and time permits, consider the following:
Inside
   - Shut off gas at the meter. Turn off pilot lights.
   - Open fireplace damper. Close fireplace screens.

- Close windows, vents, doors, blinds or noncombustible window coverings and heavy drapes.
- Remove flammable drapes and curtains.
- Move flammable furniture into the center of the home away from windows and sliding-glass doors.
- Close all interior doors and windows to prevent drafts.
- Place valuables that will not be damaged by water in a pool or pond.
- Gather pets into one room. Make plans to care for your pets if you must evacuate.
- Back your car into the garage or park it in an open space facing the direction of escape. Shut doors, and roll up windows. Leave the key in the ignition and the car doors unlocked. Close garage windows and doors, but leave them unlocked. Disconnect automatic garage door openers.

Outside
- Seal attic and ground vents with pre-cut plywood or commercial seals.
- Turn off propane tanks.
- Place combustible patio furniture inside.
- Connect garden hose to outside taps. Place lawn sprinklers on the roof and near aboveground fuel tanks. Wet the roof.
- Wet or remove shrubs within 15 feet of the home.
- Gather fire tools, such as a rake, axe, handsaw or chainsaw, bucket and shovel.

8. If advised to evacuate, do so immediately. Choose a route away from the fire hazard. Watch for changes in the speed and direction of fire and smoke.

9. See the "Evacuation" section for detailed information about evacuation preparedness. Also see the "Recovering from Disaster" and "Shelters" sections for additional information.

Chapter Twelve. Technological and Man-made Hazards

There are thousands of chemicals in our homes and places of work. Some are dangerous and even more so when they get into the wrong hands. A child can die from drinking a chemical stored in a bottle under the sink; thousands could die in a bioterrorist attack on a crowded subway or a packed indoor concert.

Most hazardous chemicals have warning properties that provide a practical means for detecting a hazard and initiating protective actions. Such warning properties make chemicals perceptible; for example, vapors or gases can be perceived by the human senses (i.e., smell, sight, taste, or irritation of the eyes, skin, or respiratory tract) before serious effects occur. The distinction between perceptible and imperceptible agents is not an exact one. The concentrations at which a person can detect an odor vary from person to person, and these thresholds also vary relative to the concentration that can produce immediate, injurious effects.

Most industrial chemicals and chemical-warfare agents are readily detectable by smell. Soldiers in World Wars I and II were taught to identify, by smell, such agents as mustard, phosgene, and chlorine, and this detection method proved effective for determining when to put on and take off a gas mask. An exception is the chemical-warfare agent Sarin, which is odorless and colorless in its pure form and, therefore, imperceptible. Japanese terrorists used Sarin when they attacked morning rush-hour commuters on several Tokyo subway trains in 1995. Twelve people died and hundreds more were injured, many of them permanently. Two years ago, police in London foiled a plot to release Sarin among the spectators of a major soccer game.

Among the most common toxic industrial chemicals, carbon monoxide is one of the few that is imperceptible. Because it is odorless and colorless, it causes many deaths in buildings each year.

Biological agents are also imperceptible and there are no detection devices that can determine their presence in the air in real time, which is why a bioterrorist attack could be so devastating. Current methods for detecting bacterial spores, such as anthrax, require a trained operator and expensive equipment. It is not currently possible to base protective responses to biological agents on detection.

Chemical incidents are characterized by the rapid onset (minutes to hours) of medical symptoms and easily observed indicators (e.g., colored residue, dead foliage, pungent odor, and dead animals, birds, fish, or insects).

In the case of a biological incident, the onset of symptoms takes days to weeks and, typically, there will be no characteristic indicators. Because of the delayed onset of symptoms in a biological incident, the area affected may be greater due to the migration of infected individuals.

Hazardous Materials Incidents

From industrial chemicals and toxic waste to household detergents and air fresheners, hazardous materials are part of our everyday lives. Affecting urban, suburban and rural areas, hazardous-materials incidents can range from a chemical spill on a highway to groundwater contamination by naturally occurring methane gas.

Hazardous materials are substances that, because of their chemical nature, pose a potential risk to life, health or property if they are released. Hazards can exist during production, storage, transportation, use or disposal.

Chemical plants are one source of hazardous materials, but there are many others. Your local service station stores gasoline and diesel fuel, hospitals store a range of radioactive and flammable materials, and there are about 30,000 hazardous-materials waste sites in the country.

Many communities have Local Emergency Planning Committees (LEPCs) that identify industrial hazardous materials and keep the community informed of the potential risk. All companies that have hazardous chemicals must report annually to the LEPC. The public is encouraged to participate in the process.

Contact your local emergency management office to find out if your community has an LEPC and how you can participate.

What to do Before a Hazardous-materials Incident

1. Ask your fire or police department about warning procedures. These could include:

- Outdoor warning sirens or horns
- Emergency Alert System (EAS) – Information provided via radio and television
- "All-Call" telephoning – An automated system for sending recorded messages
- News media – Radio, television and cable
- Residential route alerting – Messages announced to neighborhoods from vehicles equipped with public-address systems

2. Ask your LEPC or emergency management office about community plans for responding to a hazardous-materials accident at a plant or other facility, or a transportation accident involving hazardous materials.

3. Ask your LEPC about storage and usage of hazardous chemicals in your local area.

4. Use the information gathered from LEPC and local emergency management offices to evaluate risks to your household. Determine how close you are to factories, freeways, or railroads that may produce or transport toxic waste.

5. Be prepared to evacuate. An evacuation could last for a few hours or several days. See the "Evacuation" and "Emergency Planning and Disaster Supplies" sections for important information.

6. Be prepared to shelter in place; that is, to seek safety in your home or any other building you might be in at the time of a chemical release. At home you should select a room to be used as a shelter. The shelter room for use in

case of a hazardous-material incident should be above ground, large enough to accommodate all household members and pets, and should have the fewest possible exterior doors and windows. You should also assemble a shelter kit to be used to seal the shelter room during a chemical release. The kit should include plastic sheeting, duct tape, scissors, a towel, and modeling clay or other material to stuff into cracks.

What to do During a Hazardous-materials Incident

1. If you witness (or smell) a hazardous materials accident, call 911, your local emergency notification number or the fire department as soon as safely possible.

2. If you hear a warning signal, listen to local radio or television stations for further information. Follow instructions carefully.

3. Stay away from the incident site to minimize the risk of contamination.

4. If you are caught outside during an incident, remember that gases and mists are generally heavier than air. Try to stay upstream, uphill and upwind – hazardous materials can quickly be transported by water and wind. In general, try to go at least one-half mile (10 city blocks) from the danger area; for many incidents you will need to go much further.

5. If you are in a motor vehicle, stop and seek shelter in a permanent building if possible. If you must remain in your car, keep car windows and vents closed, and shut off the air conditioner and heater.

6. If asked to evacuate your home, do so immediately:

- If authorities indicate there is enough time, close all windows, shut vents and turn off attic, heating and air conditioning fans to minimize contamination.
- See the "Evacuation" section for more information.

7. If you are requested to stay indoors – shelter in place – rather than evacuate:

- Follow all instructions given by emergency authorities.

- Get household members and pets inside as quickly as possible.
- Close and lock all exterior doors and windows. Close vents, fireplace dampers and as many interior doors as possible.
- Turn off air conditioners and ventilation systems. In large buildings, the building superintendent should set all ventilation systems to 100-percent recirculation, so that no outside air is drawn into the building. If this is not possible, ventilation systems should be turned off.
- Go into the pre-selected shelter room (the above-ground room with the fewest openings to the outside). Take a battery-powered radio, water, sanitary supplies, a flashlight, and the shelter kit containing plastic sheeting, duct tape, scissors, a towel, and modeling clay or other materials to stuff into cracks.
- Close doors and windows in the room. Stuff a towel tightly under each door and tape around the sides and top of the door. Cover each window and vent in the room with a single piece of plastic sheeting, taping all around the edges of the sheeting to provide a continuous seal. If there are any cracks or holes in the room, such as those around pipes entering a bathroom, fill them with modeling clay or other similar material.
- Remain in the room, listening to emergency broadcasts on the radio, until authorities advise you to leave your shelter.
- If authorities warn of the possibility of an outdoor explosion, close all drapes, curtains, and shades in the room. Stay away from windows to prevent injury from breaking glass.
- When authorities advise people in your area to leave their shelters, open all doors and windows and turn on air conditioning and ventilation systems. These measures will flush out any chemicals that infiltrated into the building.
- See the "Shelter" section for more information.

8. Schools and other public buildings may institute procedures to shelter in place. If there is a hazardous materials incident and your children are at school, you will probably not be permitted to drive to the school to pick up your children. Even if you go to the school, the doors will probably be locked

to keep your children safe. Follow the directions of your local emergency officials.

9. Avoid contact with spilled liquids, airborne mists or condensed solid chemical deposits. Keep your body fully covered to provide some protection. Wear gloves, socks, shoes, pants and long sleeved shirts.

10. Do not eat or drink food or water that may have been contaminated.

11. If indoors, fill the bathtub (first sterilize it with a diluted bleach solution – one part bleach to 10 parts water) and large containers with water for drinking, cooking, and dishwashing. Be prepared to turn off the main water intake valve in case authorities advise you to do so.

What to do After an Incident

1. Do not return home until local authorities say it is safe.

2. Upon returning home, open windows, vents and turn on fans to provide ventilation.

3. A person or item that has been exposed to a hazardous chemical may be contaminated and could contaminate other people or items. If you have come in contact with or have been exposed to hazardous chemicals, you should:

- Follow decontamination instructions from local authorities. (Depending on the chemical, you may be advised to take a thorough shower, or you may be advised to stay away from water and follow another procedure.)
- Seek medical treatment for unusual symptoms as soon as possible.
- If medical help is not immediately available and you think you might be contaminated, remove all of your clothing and shower thoroughly (unless local authorities say the chemical is water reactive and advise you to do otherwise). Change into fresh, loose clothing and seek medical help as soon as possible.

- Place exposed clothing and shoes in tightly sealed containers. Do not allow them to contact other materials. Call local authorities to find out about proper disposal.
- Advise everyone who comes in contact with you that you may have been exposed to a toxic substance.

4. Find out from local authorities how to clean up your land and property.

5. Report any lingering vapors or other hazards to your local emergency services office.

6. See the "Recovering from Disaster" and "Shelter" sections for more information.

Household Chemical Emergencies

Nearly every household uses products containing hazardous materials. Although the risk of a chemical accident is slight, knowing how to handle these products and how to react during an emergency can reduce the risk of injury.

How to Prepare for Household Chemical Emergencies

1. Contact agencies with expertise on hazardous household materials, such as your local public health department or the Environmental Protection Agency, for information about potentially dangerous household products and their antidotes. Ask about the advisability of maintaining antidotes in your home for: cleaners and germicides, deodorizers, detergents, drain and bowl cleaners, gases, home medications, laundry bleaches, liquid fuels, paint removers and thinners.

2. Follow instructions on the product label for proper disposal of chemicals. Proper disposal will ensure environmental and public health, as well as household well-being. If you have additional questions on chemical disposal, call your local environmental or recycling agency.

- Small amounts of the following products can be safely poured down the drain with plenty of water: bathroom and glass cleaner, bleach, drain cleaner, household disinfectant, laundry and dishwashing

detergent, rubbing alcohol, rug and upholstery cleaner and toilet bowl cleaner.
- Small amounts of the following products should be disposed by wrapping the container in newspaper and plastic and placing it in the trash: brake fluid, car wax or polish, dish and laundry soap, fertilizer, furniture and floor polish, insect repellent, nail polish, oven cleaner, paint thinners and strippers, pesticides, powder cleansers, water-based paint and wood preservatives.
- Dispose of the following products at a recycling center or a collection site: kerosene, motor or fuel oil, car battery or battery acid, diesel fuel, transmission fluid, large amounts of paint, thinner or stripper, power-steering fluid, turpentine, gun cleaning solvents and tires.
- Empty spray cans completely before placing in the trash. Do not place spray cans into a burning barrel, incinerator, or trash compactor because they may explode.
- Flush outdated and unused medicines down the toilet and place the empty container in the trash. Outdated medicines can cause ill effects. Flushing will eliminate the risk of people or animals picking them out of the trash.

3. Read directions before using a new chemical product, and be sure to store household chemicals according to the instructions on the label.

4. Store chemicals in a safe, secure location, preferably up high and always out of the reach of children.

5. Avoid mixing household chemical products. Deadly toxic fumes can result from the mixture of chemicals, such as chlorine bleach and ammonia.

6. Never smoke while using household chemicals. Avoid using hair spray, cleaning solutions, paint products, or pesticides near an open flame, pilot light, lighted candle, fireplace, wood burning stove, etc. Although you may not be able to see or smell them, vapor particles in the air could catch fire or explode.

7. If you spill a chemical, clean it up immediately with rags. Be careful to protect your eyes and skin, wear gloves and eye protection. Allow the fumes

in the rags to evaporate outdoors, and then dispose of the rags by wrapping them in a newspaper and placing them in a sealed plastic bag in your trashcan.

8. Buy only as much of a chemical as you think you will use. If you have product left over, try to give it to someone who will use it. Storing hazardous chemicals increases the risk of chemical emergencies.

9. Keep an A-B-C rated fire extinguisher in the home and car, and get training from your local fire department on how to use it.

10. Post the number of the nearest poison control center by all telephones. In an emergency situation you may not have time to look up critical phone numbers.

11. Learn to detect hazardous materials. Many hazardous materials do not have a taste or an odor, and some can be detected because they cause physical reactions, such as watering eyes or nausea. Other hazardous materials exist beneath the ground and can be recognized by an oil or foam-like appearance.

12. Learn to recognize the symptoms of toxic poisoning:

- Difficulty breathing
- Irritation of the eyes, skin, throat or respiratory tract
- Changes in skin color
- Headache or blurred vision
- Dizziness
- Clumsiness or lack of coordination
- Cramps or diarrhea

What to do During a Household Chemical Emergency

1. If your child should eat or drink a non-food substance, find any containers immediately and take them to the phone. Medical professionals may need specific information from the container to give you the best emergency advice.

2. Call the poison control center, emergency medical services (EMS), 911, hospital emergency room, county health department, fire department or your local pharmacy. They will give you emergency advice while you wait for professional help. You should have such numbers on hand for easy access and use.

3. Follow the emergency operator or dispatcher's instructions carefully. The first-aid advice found on containers may not be appropriate. Do not give anything by mouth until medical professionals have advised you.

4. Take immediate action if the chemical gets into the eyes. Delaying first aid can greatly increase the likelihood of injury. Flush the eye with clear, water for a minimum of 15 minutes, unless authorities instruct you not to use water on the particular chemical involved. Continue the cleansing process even if the victim indicates he or she is no longer feeling any pain, and then seek medical attention.

5. Get out of the residence immediately if there is danger of a fire or explosion. Do not waste time collecting items or calling the fire department when you are in danger.

6. If there is a fire or explosion, call the fire department from outside (a cellular phone or a neighbor's phone) once you are safely away from danger.

7. Stay upwind and away from the residence to avoid breathing toxic fumes.

8. Wash hands, arms, or other exposed body parts that may have been exposed to the chemical. Chemicals may continue to irritate the skin until they are washed off.

9. Discard clothing that may have been contaminated. Some chemicals may not wash out completely. Discarding clothes will prevent potential future exposure.

10. Administer first-aid treatment to victims of chemical burns:

- Call 911 for emergency help.
- Remove clothing and jewelry from around the injury.

- Pour clean, cool water over the burn for 15 to 30 minutes.
- Loosely cover the burn with a sterile or clean dressing. Be sure that the dressing will not stick to the burn.
- Refer the victim to a medical professional for further treatment.

Nuclear Power Plants

Nuclear power plants operate in most states in the country and produce about 20 percent of the nation's power. Nearly three million Americans live within 10 miles of an operating nuclear power plant. Although the construction and operation of these facilities are closely monitored and regulated by the Nuclear Regulatory Commission (NRC), accidents at these plants are possible. An accident could result in dangerous levels of radiation that could affect the health and safety of the public living near the nuclear power plant.

Local and state governments, federal agencies and the electric utilities have emergency response plans in the event of a nuclear power plant incident. The plans define two "emergency planning zones." One covers an area within a 10-mile radius of the plant where it is possible that people could be harmed by direct radiation exposure. The second zone covers a broader area, usually up to a 50-mile radius from the plant, where radioactive materials could contaminate water supplies, food crops and livestock.

Understanding Radiation

Radioactive materials are composed of atoms that are unstable. An unstable atom gives off its excess energy until it becomes stable. The energy emitted is radiation. Each of us is exposed to radiation daily from natural sources, including the sun and earth. Small traces of radiation are present in food and water. Radiation also is released from man-made sources such as X-ray machines, television sets and microwave ovens. Nuclear power plants use the heat generated from nuclear fission in a contained environment to convert water to steam, which powers generators to produce electricity.

Radiation has a cumulative effect. The longer a person is exposed to radiation, the greater the risk. A high exposure to radiation can cause serious illness or death. The potential danger from an accident at a nuclear power plant is exposure to radiation. This exposure could come from the release of radioactive material from the plant into the environment, usually characterized by a plume (cloud-like) formation of radioactive gases and particles. The area that the radioactive release may affect is determined by the amount released from the plant, wind direction and speed, and weather conditions. The major hazards to people in the vicinity of the plume are radiation exposure to the body from the cloud and particles deposited on the ground, inhalation of radioactive materials and ingestion of radioactive materials.

If an accident at a nuclear power plant were to release radiation in your area, local authorities would activate warning sirens or another approved alerting method. They would also instruct you through the Emergency Alert System (EAS) on local television and radio stations on how to protect yourself.

The three ways to minimize radiation exposure are distance, shielding and time:

- Distance. The more distance between you and the source of the radiation the better. In a serious nuclear power plant accident, local authorities will call for an evacuation to increase the distance between you and the radiation.
- Shielding. As with distance, the more heavy, dense material between you and the source of the radiation the better. This is why local authorities could advise you to remain indoors if an accident occurs at a nearby nuclear power plant. In some cases, the walls in your home would be sufficient shielding to protect you.
- Time. Usually, radioactivity loses its strength fairly quickly. In a nuclear power-plant accident, local authorities will monitor any release of radiation and determine when the threat has passed.

What to do Before a Nuclear Power Plant Emergency

1. Know the terms used to describe a nuclear emergency:

Notification of Unusual Event – A small problem has occurred at the plant. No radiation leak is expected. Federal, state and county officials will be told right away. No action on your part will be necessary.

Alert – A small problem has occurred, and small amounts of radiation could leak inside the plant. This will not affect you. You should not have to do anything.

Site Area Emergency – A more serious problem. Small amounts of radiation could leak from the plant. If necessary, state and county officials will act to ensure public safety. Area sirens may be sounded. Listen to your radio or television for safety information.

General Emergency – The most serious problem. Radiation could leak outside the plant and off the plant site. The sirens will sound. Tune to your local radio or television station for reports. State and county officials will act to protect the public. Be prepared to follow instructions promptly.

2. Learn your community's warning system. Nuclear power plants are required to install sirens and other warning systems (flash warning lights) to cover a 10-mile area around the plant.

- Find out when the warning systems will be tested next.
- When tested in your area, determine whether you can hear and/or see sirens and flash warning lights from your home.

3. Obtain public emergency information materials from the power company that operates your local nuclear power plant or your local emergency services office. If you live within 10 miles of the power plant, you should receive these materials yearly from the power company or your state or local government.

4. Learn the emergency plans for schools, day-care centers, nursing homes and other places where members of your household frequent. Learn where people would go in case of evacuation. Stay tuned to your local radio and television stations.

5. Be prepared to evacuate:

- Prepare an emergency evacuation supply kit (see the "Emergency Planning and Disaster Supplies" section).
- Consider your transportation options. If you do not own or drive a car, ask your local emergency manager about plans for people without private vehicles. (See the "Evacuation" section for important details.)

What to do During a Nuclear Power Plant Emergency

1. Listen to the warning. Not all incidents result in the release of radiation. The incident could be contained inside the plant and pose no danger to the public.

2. Stay tuned to local radio or television. Local authorities will provide specific instructions and information:

- The advice given will depend on the nature of the emergency, how quickly it is evolving and how much radiation, if any, is likely to be released.
- Local instructions should take precedence over any advice given in this handbook.
- Review the public information materials you received from the power company or government officials.

3. Evacuate if you are advised to do so:

- Close and lock doors and windows.
- Keep car windows and vents closed; use re-circulating air.
- Listen to radio for evacuation routes and other instructions.
- See the "Evacuation" section for important details.

4. If you are not advised to evacuate, remain indoors:

- **Close** doors and windows.
- Turn off the air conditioner, ventilation fans, furnace and other air intakes.
- Go to a basement or other underground area, if possible.
- Keep a battery-powered radio with you at all times.

5. Shelter livestock and give them stored feed, if time permits.

6. Do not use the telephone unless absolutely necessary. Lines will be needed for emergency calls.

7. If you suspect exposure, take a thorough shower:

- Change clothes and shoes.
- Put exposed clothing in a plastic bag.
- Seal the bag and place it out of the way.

8. Put food in covered containers or in the refrigerator. Food not previously covered should be washed before being put in containers.

What to do After a Nuclear Power Plant Emergency

1. If told to evacuate, do not return home until local authorities say it is safe.

2. If you were advised to stay in your home, do not go outside until local authorities indicate it is safe.

3. Seek medical treatment for any unusual symptoms, such as nausea, that may be related to radiation exposure.

4. See the "Shelter" and "Recovering from Disaster" sections for more information.

Chapter Thirteen. National Security Emergencies

In addition to the natural and technological hazards described in this publication, Americans face threats posed by hostile governments or extremist groups. These threats to national security include acts of terrorism and acts of war.

The following is general information about national security emergencies. For more information about how to prepare for them, including volunteering in a Citizen Corps program, see the "For More Information" chapter at the end of this guide.

Terrorism

Terrorism is the use of force or violence against people or property in violation of the criminal laws of the United States for purposes of intimidation, coercion or ransom. Terrorists often use threats to create fear among the public, to try to convince citizens that their government is powerless to prevent terrorism and to get immediate publicity for their causes.

Acts of terrorism can range from threats of terrorism to assassinations, kidnappings, hijackings, cyber-attacks (computer-based), bomb scares and bombings, and the use of chemical, biological and nuclear weapons.

High-risk targets include military and civilian government facilities, international airports, large cities and high-profile landmarks. Terrorists might also target large public gatherings, water and food supplies, utilities and corporate centers. Further, they are capable of spreading fear by sending explosives or chemical and biological agents through the mail.

In the immediate area of a terrorist event, you would need to rely on police, fire and other officials for instructions. However, you can prepare in much the same way you would prepare for other crisis events.

Preparing for Terrorism
1. Wherever you are, be aware of your surroundings. The very nature of terrorism suggests there may be little or no warning.

2. Take precautions when traveling. Be aware of conspicuous or unusual behavior. Do not accept packages from strangers. Do not leave luggage unattended. Unusual behavior, suspicious packages and strange devices should be promptly reported to the police or security personnel.

3. Do not be afraid to move or leave if you feel uncomfortable or if something does not seem right.

4. Learn where emergency exits are located in buildings you frequent. When you enter unfamiliar buildings, notice where exits and staircases are located. Plan how to get out of a building, subway or congested public area or traffic. Notice heavy or breakable objects that could move, fall or break in an explosion.

5. Assemble a disaster supply kit at home and learn first aid. Separate the supplies you would take if you had to evacuate quickly, and put them in a backpack or container, ready to go.

6. Be familiar with different types of fire extinguishers and how to locate them. Know the location and availability of hard hats in buildings in which you spend a lot of time.

Protection against Cyber Attacks

Cyber-attacks target computer or telecommunication networks of critical infrastructures, such as power systems, traffic-control systems or financial systems. Cyber-attacks target information technologies (IT) in three different ways. First, is a direct attack against an information system "through the wires" alone (hacking). Second, the attack can be a physical assault against a critical IT element. Third, the attack can be from the inside as a result of compromising a trusted party with access to the system.

1. Be prepared to do without services you normally depend on that could be disrupted – electricity, telephone, natural gas, gasoline pumps, cash registers, ATM machines and Internet transactions.

2. Be prepared to respond to official instructions if a cyber-attack triggers other hazards, for example, general evacuation, evacuation to shelter, or shelter in place, because of hazardous-materials releases, nuclear power plant incident, dam or flood-control system failures.

Preparing for a Building Explosion

Explosions can collapse buildings and cause fires. People who live or work in a multi-level building can do the following:

1. Review emergency evacuation procedures. Know where emergency exits are located.

2. Keep fire extinguishers in working order. Know where they are located, and learn how to use them.

3. Learn first aid. Contact the local chapter of the American Red Cross for information and training.

4. Building owners should keep the following items in a designated place on each floor of the building:
- Portable, battery-operated radio and extra batteries
- Several flashlights and extra batteries
- First aid kit and manual
- Several hard hats
- Fluorescent tape to rope off dangerous areas

Bomb Threats

If you receive a bomb threat, get as much information from the caller as possible. Keep the caller on the line and record everything that is said. Then notify the police and the building management. If you are notified of a bomb threat, do not touch any suspicious packages. Clear the area around suspicious packages, and notify the police immediately. In evacuating a building, don't stand in front of windows, glass doors or other potentially hazardous areas. Do not block sidewalk or streets to be used by emergency officials or others still exiting the building.

Suspicious Parcels and Letters

Be wary of suspicious packages and letters. They can contain explosives, chemical or biological agents. Be particularly cautious at your place of employment. Some typical characteristics postal inspectors have detected over the years, which ought to trigger suspicion, include parcels that:
- Are unexpected or from someone unfamiliar to you
- Have no return address, or have one that can't be verified as legitimate
- Are marked with restrictive endorsements, such as "Personal," "Confidential" or "Do not X-ray"
- Have protruding wires or aluminum foil, strange odors or stains
- Show a city or state in the postmark that doesn't match the return address
- Are of unusual weight, given their size, or are lopsided or oddly shaped
- Are marked with any threatening language
- Have inappropriate or unusual labeling

- Have excessive postage or excessive packaging material, such as masking tape and string
- Have misspellings of common words
- Are addressed to someone no longer with your organization or are otherwise outdated
- Have incorrect titles or title without a name
- Are not addressed to a specific person
- Have handwritten or poorly typed addresses

With suspicious envelopes and packages other than those that might contain explosives, take these additional steps against possible biological and chemical agents:
- Refrain from eating or drinking in a designated mail-handling area.
- Place suspicious envelopes or packages in a plastic bag or some other type of container to prevent leakage of contents. Never sniff or smell suspect mail.
- If you do not have a container, then cover the envelope or package with anything available (e.g., clothing, paper, trashcan, etc.) and do not remove the cover.
- Leave the room and close the door, or section off the area to prevent others from entering.
- Wash your hands with soap and water to prevent spreading any powder to your face.
- If you are at work, report the incident to your building security official or an available supervisor, who should notify police and other authorities without delay.
- List all people who were in the room or area when this suspicious letter or package was recognized. Give a copy of this list to both the local public health authorities and law enforcement officials for follow-up investigations and advice.
- If you are at home, report the incident to local police.

What to do When There is an Explosion
Leave the building as quickly as possible. Do not stop to retrieve personal possessions or make phone calls. If things are falling around you, get under a sturdy table or desk until they stop falling. Then leave quickly, watching for weakened floors and stairs and falling debris as you exit.
1. If there is a fire:
    - Stay low to the floor and exit the building as quickly as possible.
    - Cover your nose and mouth with a wet cloth.

- When approaching a closed door, use the back of your hand to feel the lower, middle and upper parts of the door. Never use the palm of your hand or fingers to test for heat: burning those areas could impair your ability to escape a fire (i.e., ladders and crawling).
- If the door is NOT hot, open slowly and ensure fire and/or smoke is not blocking your escape route. If your escape route is blocked, shut the door immediately and use an alternate escape route, such as a window. If clear, leave immediately through the door. Be prepared to crawl. Smoke and heat rise. The air is clearer and cooler near the floor.
- If the door is hot, do not open it. Escape through a window. If you cannot escape, hang a white or light-colored sheet outside the window, alerting fire fighters of your presence.
- Heavy smoke and poisonous gases collect first along the ceiling. Stay below the smoke at all times.

2. If you are trapped in debris:
   - Do not light a match.
   - Do not move about or kick up dust. Cover your mouth with a handkerchief or clothing.
   - Rhythmically tap on a pipe or wall so that rescuers can hear where you are. Use a whistle if one is available. Shout only as a last resort when you hear sounds and think someone will hear you – shouting can cause a person to inhale dangerous amounts of dust.

Chemical and Biological Weapons

In case of a chemical or biological weapon attack near you, authorities will instruct you on the best course of action. This may be to evacuate the area immediately, to seek shelter at a designated location, or to take immediate shelter where you are and seal the premises. To best protect yourself, take emergency preparedness measures ahead of time and to get medical attention as soon as possible, if needed.

INDICATIONS OF CBR CONTAMINATION

Researchers are working on a prototype device to automatically and continuously monitor the air for the presence of bacterial spores. The device would continuously sample the air and use microwaves to trigger a chemical reaction, the intensity of which would correspond to the concentration of bacterial spores in the sample. If an increase in spore concentration is detected, an alarm similar to a smoke detector would sound and a technician would respond and use traditional sampling and analysis to confirm the presence of anthrax spores.

In the absence of a warning, people can be alerted to some airborne hazards by observing symptoms or effects in others. This provides a practical means for initiating protective actions, because the susceptibility to hazardous materials varies from person to person. The concentrations of airborne materials may also vary substantially within a given building or room, producing a hazard that may be greater to some occupants than to others.

Other warning signs of a hazard may involve seeing and hearing something out of the ordinary, such as the hiss of a rapid release from a pressurized cylinder. Awareness to warning properties, signs, and symptoms in other people is the basis of a protective action plan. Such a plan should apply four possible protective actions: sheltering in place, using protective masks, evacuating, and purging, as already discussed.

For protection against imperceptible agents, the only practical protective measures are those that are continuously in place, such as filtering all air brought into the building on a continuous basis and using automatic, real-time sensors that are capable of detecting the imperceptible agents.

Chemical, biological, and radiological materials, as well as industrial agents, may travel in the air as a gas or on surfaces we physically contact. Dispersion methods may be as simple as placing a container in a heavily used area, opening a container, or using conventional (garden)/commercial spray devices, or as elaborate as detonating an aerosol. Chemical incidents are characterized by the rapid onset (minutes to hours) of medical symptoms and easily observed indicators (e.g., dead foliage, pungent odor, and dead animals, birds, fish, or insects.

Signs of Chemical Threat

Many sick or dead birds, fish or small animals are cause for suspicion – not just an occasional road kill, but numerous animals (wild and domestic, small and large), birds, and fish in the same area.

Lack of insect life – if normal insect activity (ground, air, and/or water) is missing, check the ground/water surface/shore line for dead insects. If near water, check for dead fish/aquatic birds.

Physical symptoms – numerous individuals experiencing unexplained water-like blisters, wheals (like bee stings), pinpointed pupils, choking, respiratory ailments, and/or rashes.

Mass casualties – many individuals exhibiting unexplained serious health problems, ranging from nausea to disorientation to difficulty in breathing to convulsions to death.

Definite pattern of casualties – casualties distributed in a pattern that may be associated with possible agent dissemination methods.

Illness associated with confined geographic area – lower attack rates for people working indoors than those working outdoors and vice versa.

Unusual liquid droplets – numerous surfaces exhibit oily droplets/film; numerous water surfaces have an oily film. (No recent rain.)

Areas that look different – not just a patch of dead weeds, but trees, shrubs, bushes, food crops, and/or lawns that are dead, discolored, or withered. (No current drought.)

Unexplained odors – smells may range from fruity to flowery to sharp/pungent to garlic/horseradish-like to bitter almonds/peach kernels to new mown hay. It is important to note that the particular odor is completely out of character with its surroundings.

Low-lying clouds – a low-lying cloud/fog-like condition that is not explained by its surroundings.

Unusual metal debris – an unexplained bomb/munitions-like material, especially if it contains a liquid. (No recent rain.)

If You See Signs of Chemical Attack: Find Clean Air Quickly

Quickly try to **define the impacted area** or where the chemical is coming from, if possible.

Take immediate action to **get away**.

If the chemical is inside a building where you are, get out of the building without passing through the contaminated area, if possible.

If you can't get out of the building or find clean air without passing through the area where you see signs of a chemical attack, it may be better to move as far away as possible and "shelter in place."

If you are outside, quickly decide what is the fastest way to find clean air. Consider if you can get out of the area or if you should go inside the closest building and "shelter in place."

If You Think You Have Been Exposed to a Chemical

If your eyes are watering, your skin is stinging, and you are having trouble breathing, you may have been exposed to a chemical.

If you think you may have been **exposed to a chemical, strip immediately** and **wash**.

Look for a hose, fountain, or any source of **water**, and wash with **soap** if possible, being sure not to scrub the chemical into your skin.

Seek emergency **medical attention**.

Bioterrorism

Bioterrorism poses an enormous threat and is difficult to prevent. A small vial of anthrax or smallpox could be released and cause tens of thousands of casualties. Terrorists are most likely to use organisms that cause infectious diseases because they are easily spread among people.
Biological agents include bacteria, viruses, and rickettsia.

Toxins, which are poisons of biological origin and not living organisms, are sometimes grouped with biological agents and sometimes with chemical agents. Although there are hundreds of microorganisms that could be used as biological agents, the likely number is much smaller when the agents' effectiveness, reliability, availability, ease of manufacture, and stability in storage and dissemination are considered.

When disseminated as aerosols, biological agents are most effective in the size range of 1 to 5 microns, because they can remain suspended for long periods. Smaller particles are less likely to survive as aerosols, and larger particles settle rapidly, making them less likely to enter the lungs.

Anthrax

The death rate for anthrax from inhaled sources is very high, approaching 100 percent. Death rates are lower for anthrax that enters your body through food or a wound. Anthrax is easy to produce, and it's readily available around the world. The spores don't require special handling procedures, so terrorists could take anthrax to many points for distribution. Unlike many disease-causing bacteria, spores can survive severe heat and cold.]

Anthrax is an acute infectious disease caused by the spore-forming bacterium Bacillus anthracis. Anthrax most commonly occurs in hoofed mammals and can also infect humans.

Symptoms of disease vary depending on how the disease was contracted, but usually occur within 7 days after exposure. The serious forms of human anthrax are inhalation anthrax, cutaneous anthrax, and intestinal anthrax.

Initial symptoms of inhalation anthrax infection may resemble a common cold. After several days, the symptoms may progress to severe breathing problems and shock. Inhalation anthrax is often fatal.

The intestinal disease form of anthrax may follow the consumption of contaminated food and is characterized by an acute inflammation of the intestinal tract. Initial signs of nausea, loss of appetite, vomiting, and fever are followed by abdominal pain, vomiting of blood, and severe diarrhea.

Direct person-to-person spread of anthrax is extremely unlikely, if it occurs at all. Therefore, there is no need to immunize or treat contacts of persons ill with anthrax, such as household contacts, friends, or coworkers, unless they also were also exposed to the same source of infection.

In persons exposed to anthrax, infection can be prevented with antibiotic treatment. Early antibiotic treatment of anthrax is essential; delay lessens chances for survival. Anthrax usually is susceptible to penicillin, doxycycline, and fluoroquinolones. An anthrax vaccine also can prevent infection. Vaccination against anthrax is not recommended for the general public to prevent disease and is not available.

Smallpox
About 30 percent of those infected with smallpox die of it. Many people have never been vaccinated for smallpox, and no one knows whether those who received vaccinations 25 or more years ago are still protected. Smallpox is harder to propagate than anthrax and less tolerant of severe conditions. However, it can spread very rapidly from person to person.

Smallpox is a serious, contagious, and sometimes fatal infectious disease. There is no specific treatment for smallpox disease, and the only prevention is vaccination. The name smallpox is derived from the Latin word for "spotted" and refers to the raised bumps that appear on the face and body of an infected person.

There are two clinical forms of smallpox. Variola major is the severe and most common form of smallpox, with a more extensive rash and higher fever. There are four types of variola major Oth(mild and occurring in previously vaccinated persons); flat; and hemorrhagic (both rare and very severe). Historically, variola major has an overall fatality rate of about 30%; however, flat and hemorrhagic smallpox usually are fatal. Variola minor is a less common presentation of smallpox, and a much less severe disease, with death rates historically of 1% or less.

Smallpox outbreaks have occurred from time to time for thousands of years, but the disease is now eradicated after a successful worldwide vaccination program. The last case of smallpox in the United States was in 1949. The last naturally occurring case in the world was in Somalia in 1977. After the disease was eliminated from the world, routine vaccination against smallpox among the general public was stopped because it was no longer necessary for prevention.

Where Smallpox Comes From

Smallpox is caused by the variola virus that emerged in human populations thousands of years ago. Except for laboratory stockpiles, the variola virus has been eliminated. However, in the aftermath of the events of September and October, 2001, there is heightened concern that the variola virus might be used as an agent of bioterrorism. For this reason, the U.S. government is taking precautions for dealing with a smallpox outbreak.

Transmission

Generally, direct and fairly prolonged face-to-face contact is required to spread smallpox from one person to another. Smallpox also can be spread through direct contact with infected bodily fluids or contaminated objects such as bedding or clothing. Rarely, smallpox has been spread by virus carried in the air in enclosed settings such as buildings, buses, and trains. Humans are the only natural hosts of variola. Smallpox is not known to be transmitted by insects or animals. A person with smallpox is sometimes contagious with onset of fever (prodrome phase), but the person becomes most contagious with the onset of rash. At this stage the infected person is usually very sick and not able to move around in the community. The infected person is contagious until the last smallpox scab falls off.

Other threats

Other infectious diseases that pose a threat include plague, tularemia, botulism, viral hemorrhagic fever and tuberculosis.

Botulism

Botulism is a muscle-paralyzing disease caused by a toxin made by a bacterium called Clostridium botulinum. There are three main kinds of botulism:

Foodborne botulism occurs when a person ingests pre-formed toxin that leads to illness within a few hours to days. Foodborne botulism is a public health emergency because the contaminated food may still be available to other persons besides the patient.

Infant botulism occurs in a small number of susceptible infants each year who harbor C. botulinum in their intestinal tract.

Wound botulism occurs when wounds are infected with C. botulinum that secretes the toxin.

With foodborne botulism, symptoms begin within 6 hours to 2 weeks (most commonly between 12 and 36 hours) after eating toxin-containing food. Symptoms of botulism include double vision, blurred vision, drooping eyelids, slurred speech, difficulty swallowing, dry mouth, muscle weakness that always descends through the body: first shoulders are affected, then upper arms, lower arms, thighs, calves, etc. Paralysis of breathing muscles can cause a person to stop breathing and die, unless assistance with breathing (mechanical ventilation) is provided.

Botulism is not spread from one person to another. Foodborne botulism can occur in all age groups. A supply of antitoxin against botulism is maintained by CDC. The antitoxin is effective in reducing the severity of symptoms if administered early in the course of the disease. Most patients eventually recover after weeks to months of supportive care.

However, experts believe these organisms and diseases are unlikely to cause widespread illness because they're difficult to manufacture and distribute. These organisms are also less hardy than anthrax is. Alternatively, biological toxins derived from living organisms, such as the botulinum toxin derived from the bacterium *Clostridium botulinum*, or toxins derived from plants, such as ricin, from castor beans, could be used in terrorist attacks.

The bad news is that there is little citizens can do to prepare for a bioterror attack. The best defense against widespread disease is early detection which is handled by public health authorities, and that is where resources need to be focused.

Biological
Biological agents are organisms or toxins that can kill or incapacitate people, livestock and crops. The three basic groups of biological agents that would likely be used as weapons are bacteria, viruses and toxins.
 1. Bacteria: Bacteria are small free-living organisms that reproduce by simple division and are easy to grow. The diseases they produce often respond to treatment with antibiotics.
 2. Viruses: Viruses are organisms that require living cells in which to reproduce and are intimately dependent upon the body they infect. Viruses produce diseases that generally do not respond to antibiotics. However, antiviral drugs are sometimes effective.
 3. Toxins: Toxins are poisonous substances found in, and extracted from, living plants, animals, or microorganisms; some toxins can be produced or altered by chemical means. Some toxins can be treated with specific antitoxins and selected drugs. Most biological agents are difficult to grow and maintain. Many break down quickly when exposed to sunlight and other environmental factors, while others, such as anthrax spores are very long lived. They can be dispersed by being sprayed in the air or infecting animals that carry the disease to humans, as well as through food and water contamination.

- Aerosols: Biological agents are dispersed into the air, forming a fine mist that may drift for miles. Inhaling the agent may cause disease in people or animals.
- Animals: Some insects and animals, such as fleas, mice, flies and mosquitoes, are used to spread diseases. Deliberately spreading diseases through livestock is also referred to as agroterrorism.
- Food and water contamination: Some pathogenic organisms and toxins may persist in food and water supplies. Most microbes can be killed, and toxins deactivated, by cooking food and boiling water. Anthrax spores formulated as a white powder were mailed to individuals in the government and media in the fall of 2001. Postal sorting machines and the opening of letters dispersed the spores as aerosols. Several deaths resulted. The effect was to disrupt mail services and to cause a widespread fear of handling delivered mail. Person-to-person spread of a few infectious agents is also possible. Humans have been the source of infection for smallpox, plague, and the Lassa viruses.

Chemical

Chemical warfare agents are poisonous vapors, aerosols, liquids or solids that have toxic effects on people, animals or plants. They can be released by bombs, sprayed from aircraft, boats, or vehicles, or used as a liquid to create a hazard to people and the environment. Some chemical agents may be odorless and tasteless. They can have an immediate effect (a few seconds to a few minutes) or a delayed effect (several hours to several days). While potentially lethal, chemical agents are difficult to deliver in lethal concentrations. Outdoors, the agents often dissipate rapidly. Chemical agents are also difficult to produce.

There are six types of agents:
- Lung-damaging (pulmonary) agents, such as phosgene
- Cyanide
- Vesicants or blister agents, such as mustard
- Nerve agents, such as GA (tabun), GB (sarin), GD (soman), GF, and VX
- Incapacitating agents, such as BZ
- Riot-control agents (similar to MACE)

What to do After a Chemical Attack

Immediate symptoms of exposure to chemical agents may include blurred vision, eye irritation, difficulty breathing and nausea. A person affected by a chemical or biological agent requires immediate attention by professional medical personnel. If medical help is not immediately available, decontaminate yourself and assist in decontaminating others. Decontamination is needed within minutes of exposure to minimize health consequences. However, you should not leave the safety of a shelter to go outdoors to help others until authorities announce it is safe to do so.

1. Use extreme caution when helping others who have been exposed to chemical agents:

- Remove all clothing and other items in contact with the body. Contaminated clothing normally removed over the head should be cut off to avoid contact with the eyes, nose, and mouth. Put into a plastic bag if possible. Decontaminate hands using soap and water. Remove eyeglasses or contact lenses. Put glasses in a pan of household bleach to decontaminate.

153

2. Remove all items in contact with the body.

3. Flush eyes with lots of water.

4. Gently wash face and hair with soap and water; then thoroughly rinse with water.

5. Decontaminate other body areas likely to have been contaminated. Blot – do not swab or scrape – with a cloth soaked in soapy water and rinse with clear water.

6. Change into uncontaminated clothes. Clothing stored in drawers or closets is likely to be uncontaminated.

7. If possible, proceed to a medical facility for screening.

What to do After a Biological Attack

In many biological attacks, people will not know they have been exposed to an agent. In such situations, the first evidence of an attack may be when you notice symptoms of the disease caused by an agent exposure, and you should seek immediate medical attention for treatment.

In some situations, such as the anthrax letters sent in 2001, people may be alerted to a potential exposure. If this is the case, pay close attention to all official warnings and instructions on how to proceed. The delivery of medical services for a biological event may be handled differently to respond to increased demand. Again, it will be important for you to pay attention to official instructions via radio, television and emergency alert systems.

If your skin or clothing comes in contact with a visible, potentially infectious substance, you should remove and bag your clothes and personal items and wash yourself with warm soapy water immediately. Put on clean clothes and seek medical assistance. For more information, visit the website for the Centers for Disease Control and Prevention at www.bt.cdc.gov.

Chapter Fourteen. Everyday Survival

So far we have covered emergencies in the field often far off the beaten track where you have to fend for yourself and others in your group. However, disasters can occur at any time and you should plan ahead and be prepared for them.

One of the most important steps you can take in preparing for emergencies is to develop a household disaster plan.

- Learn about the natural disasters that could occur in your community from your local emergency management office or American Red Cross chapter. Learn whether hazardous materials are produced, stored or transported near your area. Learn about possible consequences of deliberate acts of terror. Ask how to prepare for each potential emergency and how to respond.
- Talk with employers and school officials about their emergency response plans.
- Talk with your household about potential emergencies and how to respond to each. Talk about what you would need to do in an evacuation.
- Plan how your household would stay in contact if you were separated. Identify two meeting places: the first should be near your home – in case of fire, perhaps a tree or a telephone pole; the second should be away from your neighborhood in case you cannot return home.
- Pick a friend or relative, who lives out of the area, for household members to call to say they are OK.
- Draw a floor plan of your home. Mark two escape routes from each room.
- Post emergency telephone numbers by telephones. Teach children how and when to call 911.
- Make sure everyone in your household knows how and when to shut off water, gas, and electricity at the main switches. Consult with your

local utilities if you have questions. Take a first-aid and CPR class. Local American Red Cross chapters can provide information. Official certification by the American Red Cross provides "good Samaritan" law protection for those giving first aid.
- Reduce the economic impact of disaster on your property and your household's health and financial well-being.
- Review property insurance policies before disaster strikes – make sure policies are current and be certain they meet your needs (type of coverage, amount of coverage, and hazards covered – flood, earthquake).
- Protect your household's financial well-being before a disaster strikes – review life-insurance policies and consider saving money in an "emergency" savings account that could be used in any crisis. It is advisable to keep a small amount of cash or traveler's checks at home in a safe place where you can quickly gain access in case of an evacuation.
- Be certain that health insurance policies are current and meet the needs of your household.
- Consider ways to help neighbors who may need special assistance, such as the elderly or the disabled.
- Make arrangements for pets. Pets are not usually allowed in public shelters. Service animals, for those who depend on them, are allowed.

Emergency Planning for People with Special Needs

If you have a disability or special need, you may have to take additional steps to protect yourself and your household in an emergency. If you know of friends or neighbors with special needs, help them with these extra precautions. Examples include:

- Hearing impaired may need to make special arrangements to receive a warning.
- Mobility impaired may need assistance in getting to a shelter.
- Households with a single, working parent may need help from others both in planning for disasters and during an emergency.

- Non-English speaking people may need assistance planning for and responding to emergencies. Community and cultural groups may be able to help keep these populations informed.
- People without vehicles may need to make arrangements for transportation.
- People with special dietary needs should have an adequate emergency food supply.

1. Find out about special assistance that may be available in your community. Register with the office of emergency services or fire department for assistance, so needed help can be provided quickly in an emergency.

2. Create a network of neighbors, relatives, friends and co-workers to aid you in an emergency. Discuss your needs and make sure they know how to operate necessary equipment.

3. Discuss your needs with your employer.

4. If you are mobility impaired and live or work in a high-rise building, have an escape chair.

5. If you live in an apartment building, ask the management to mark accessible exits clearly and to make arrangements to help you evacuate the building.

6. Keep extra wheelchair batteries, oxygen, catheters, medication, food for seeing-eye or hearing-ear dogs, or other items you might need. Also, keep a list of the type and serial numbers of medical devices you need.

7. Those who are not disabled should learn who in their neighborhood or building is disabled, so that they may assist them during emergencies.

8. If you are a caregiver for a person with special needs, make sure you have a plan to communicate if an emergency occurs.

Disaster Supply Kits

You may need to survive on your own for three days or more. This means having your own water, food and emergency supplies. Try using backpacks or duffel bags to keep the supplies together.

Assembling the supplies you might need following a disaster is an important part of your disaster plan. You should prepare the following emergency supplies:

- Keep a disaster supply kit with essential food, water, and supplies for at least three days – this kit should be kept in a designated place and be ready to "grab and go" in case you have to leave your home quickly because of a disaster, such as a flash flood or major chemical emergency. Make sure all household members know where the kit is kept.
- Consider having additional supplies for use in shelters or home confinement for up to two weeks.
- You should also have a disaster supply kit at work. This should be in one container, ready to "grab and go" in case you have to evacuate the building.
- Keep a car kit of emergency supplies, including food and water, stored in your vehicle at all times. This kit would also include flares, jumper cables, and seasonal supplies.

The following checklists will help you assemble disaster supply kits that meet the needs of your household. The basic items that should be in a disaster supply kit are water, food, first-aid supplies, tools and emergency supplies, clothing and bedding, and specialty items. You will need to change the stored water and food supplies every six months, so be sure to write the date you store it on all containers. You should also re-think your needs every year and update your kit as your household changes. Keep items in airtight plastic bags and put your entire disaster supply kit in one or two easy-to-carry containers such as an unused trashcan, camping backpack or duffel bag.

Water: The Absolute Necessity

- Stocking water reserves should be a top priority. Drinking water in emergency situations should not be rationed. Therefore, it is critical to store adequate amounts of water for your household.
- Individual needs vary, depending on age, physical condition, activity, diet, and climate. A normally active person needs at least two quarts of water daily just for drinking. Children, nursing mothers, and ill people need more. Very hot temperatures can double the amount of water needed.
- Because you will also need water for sanitary purposes and, possibly, for cooking, you should store at least one gallon of water per person per day.
- Store water in thoroughly washed plastic, fiberglass or enamel-lined metal containers. Don't use containers that can break, such as glass bottles. Never use a container that has held toxic substances. Sound plastic containers, such as soft drinks bottles, are best. You can also purchase food-grade plastic buckets or drums.
- Containers for water should be rinsed with a diluted bleach solution (one part bleach to 10 parts water) before use. Previously used bottles or other containers may be contaminated with microbes or chemicals. Do not rely on untested devices for decontaminating water.
- If your water is treated commercially by a water utility, you do not need to treat water before storing it. Additional treatments of treated public water will not increase storage life.
- If you have a well or public water that has not been treated, follow the treatment instructions provided by your public health service or water provider.
- If you suspect that your well may be contaminated, contact your local or state health department or agriculture extension agent for specific advice.
- Seal your water containers tightly, label them and store them in a cool, dark place.

- It is important to change stored water every six months.

Food: Preparing an Emergency Supply

- If activity is reduced, healthy people can survive on half their usual food intake for an extended period or without any food for many days. Food, unlike water, may be rationed safely, except for children and pregnant women.
- You don't need to go out and buy unfamiliar foods to prepare an emergency food supply. You can use the canned goods, dry mixes and other staples on your cupboard shelves. Canned goods do not require cooking, water or special preparation. Be sure to include a manual can opener.
- Keep canned goods in a dry place where the temperature is fairly cool. To protect boxed foods from pests and to extend their shelf life, store the food in tightly closed plastic or metal containers. Replace items in your food supply every six months. Throw out any canned good that becomes swollen, dented, or corroded. Use foods before they go bad, and replace them with fresh supplies. Date each food item with a marker. Place new items at the back of the storage area and older ones in front.
- Food items that you might consider including in your disaster supply kit include: ready-to-eat meats, fruits and vegetables; canned or boxed juices, milk and soup; high-energy foods like peanut butter, jelly, low-sodium crackers, granola bars and trail mix; vitamins; foods for infants or people on special diets; cookies and hard candy; instant coffee, cereals and powdered milk.

You may need to survive on your own after a disaster. Local officials and relief workers will be on the scene after a disaster, but they cannot reach everyone immediately. You could get help in hours, or it may take days. Basic services, such as electricity, gas, water, sewage treatment and telephones, may be cut off for days, even a week or longer. Or you may have to evacuate at a moment's notice and take essentials with you. You probably won't have the opportunity to shop or search for the supplies you'll need. Your household will cope best by preparing for disaster before it strikes.

First-Aid Supplies

Assemble a first-aid kit for your home and for each vehicle. The basics for your first aid kit should include:

- First-aid manual
- Sterile adhesive bandages in assorted sizes
- Assorted sizes of safety pins
- Cleansing agents (isopropyl alcohol, hydrogen peroxide)/soap/germicide
- Antibiotic ointment
- Latex gloves (at least 2 pairs)
- Petroleum jelly
- 2-inch and 4-inch sterile gauze pads (4-6 each size)
- Triangular bandages (3)
- 2-inch and 3-inch sterile roller bandages (3 rolls each)
- Cotton balls
- Scissors
- Tweezers
- Needle
- Moistened towelettes
- Antiseptic
- Thermometer
- Tongue depressor blades (2)
- Tube of petroleum jelly or other lubricant
- Sunscreen

It may be difficult to obtain prescription medications during a disaster because stores may be closed or supplies may be limited. Ask your physician or pharmacist about storing prescription medications. Be sure they are stored to meet instructions on the label and be mindful of expirations dates¬ – be sure to keep your stored medication up to date. Have an extra pair of prescription glasses or contact lens.

Have the following nonprescription drugs in your disaster supply kit:

- Aspirin and non-aspirin pain reliever
- Anti-diarrhea medication
- Antacid (for stomach upset)
- Syrup of ipecac (use to induce vomiting if advised by the poison control center)
- Laxatives
- Vitamins

Tools and Emergency Supplies

It will be important to assemble these items in a disaster supply kit, in case you have to leave your home quickly. Even if you don't have to leave your home, if you lose power it will be easier to have these item already assembled and in one place.

Tools and other items:

- A portable, battery-powered radio or television and extra batteries (also have a NOAA weather radio, if appropriate for your area)
- Flashlight and extra batteries
- Signal flare
- Matches in a waterproof container (or waterproof matches)
- Shut-off wrench, pliers, shovel and other tools
- Duct tape and scissors
- Plastic sheeting
- Whistle
- Small canister, A-B-C-type fire extinguisher
- Tube tent
- Compass
- Work gloves
- Paper, pens and pencils
- Needles and thread
- Battery-operated travel alarm clock

Kitchen items:

- Manual can opener
- Mess kits or paper cups, plates and plastic utensils
- All-purpose knife
- Household liquid bleach to treat drinking water
- Sugar, salt and pepper
- Aluminum foil and plastic wrap
- Re-sealing plastic bags
- If food must be cooked, small cooking stove and a can of cooking fuel

Sanitation and hygiene items:

- Washcloth and towel
- Towelettes, soap, hand sanitizer and liquid detergent
- Toothpaste, toothbrushes, shampoo, deodorants, comb and brush, razor, shaving cream, lip balm, sunscreen, insect repellent, contact lens solutions, mirror and feminine supplies
- Heavy-duty plastic garbage bags and ties¬¬, for personal sanitation use
- Toilet paper
- Medium-sized plastic bucket with tight lid
- Disinfectant and household chlorine bleach
- Consider including a small shovel for digging a latrine

Household documents and contact numbers:

- Personal identification, cash (including change) or traveler's checks, and a credit card
- Copies of important documents: birth certificate, marriage certificate, driver's license, Social Security cards, passport, wills, deeds, inventory of household goods, insurance papers, immunizations records, bank and credit card account numbers, stocks and bonds (Be sure to store these in a watertight container.)

- Emergency contact list and phone numbers
- Map of the area and phone numbers of places you could go
- An extra set of car keys and house keys

Clothes and bedding:

- One complete change of clothing and footwear for each household member
- Shoes should be sturdy work shoes or boots
- Rain gear, hat and gloves, extra socks, extra underwear, thermal underwear and sunglasses
- Blankets or a sleeping bag for each household member and pillows

Specialty items:

Remember to consider the needs of infants, elderly people, disabled people and pets, and to include entertainment and comfort items for children.

- For baby
- For the elderly
- For pets
- Entertainment: books, games, quiet toys and stuffed animals

It is important for you to be ready, wherever you may be, when disaster strikes. With the checklists provided you can now put together appropriate disaster supply kits for your household:

- A disaster supply kit kept in the home with supplies for at least three days.
- Although it is unlikely that food supplies would be cut off for as long as two weeks, consider storing additional water, food, clothing, bedding and other supplies to expand your supply kit to last up to two weeks.
- A workplace disaster supply kit. (It is important to store a personal supply of water and food at work; you will not be able to rely on

water fountains or coolers. Women who wear high heels should be sure to have comfortable flat shoes at their workplace in case an evacuation requires walking long distances.)
- A car disaster supply kit. (Keep a smaller disaster supply kit in the trunk of your car. If you become stranded or are not able to return home, having these items will help you be more comfortable until help arrives. Add items for severe winter weather during months when heavy snow or icy roads are possible – salt, sand, shovels, and extra winter clothing, including hats and gloves.)

Evacuation

Evacuations are more common than many people realize. Hundreds of times each year, transportation and industrial accidents release harmful substances, forcing thousands of people to leave their homes. Fires and floods cause evacuations even more frequently. And almost every year, people along the Gulf and Atlantic coasts evacuate in the face of approaching hurricanes.

When community evacuations become necessary, local officials provide information to the public through the media. In some circumstances other warning methods, such as sirens or telephone calls, are also used.

Government agencies, the American Red Cross, Salvation Army, and other disaster relief organizations provide emergency shelter and supplies. To be prepared for an emergency, you should have enough water, food, clothing and emergency supplies to last at least three days. In a catastrophic emergency, you might need to be self-sufficient for even longer.

The amount of time you have to evacuate will depend on the disaster. If the event can be monitored, such as a hurricane, you might have a day or two to get ready. However, many disasters allow no time for people to gather even the most basic necessities. This is why you should prepare now.

Planning for Evacuation
1. Ask your local emergency management office about community evacuation plans. Learn evacuation routes. If you do not own a car, make transportation arrangements with friends or your local government.

2. Talk with your household about the possibility of evacuation. Plan where you would go if you had to leave the community. Determine how you would get there. In your planning, consider different scales of evacuations. In a hurricane, for example, entire counties would evacuate, while a much smaller area would be affected by a chemical release.

3. Plan a place to meet your household in case you are separated from one another in a disaster. Ask a friend outside your town to be the "checkpoint" so that everyone in the household can call that person to say they are safe.

4. Find out where children will be sent if schools are evacuated.

5. Assemble a disaster supplies kit. Include a battery-powered radio, flashlight, extra batteries, food, water and clothing. See the "Emergency Planning and Disaster Supplies" chapter for a complete list.

6. Keep fuel in your car if an evacuation seems likely. Gas stations may be closed during emergencies and unable to pump gas during power outages.

7. Know how to shut off your home's electricity, gas and water supplies at main switches and valves. Have the tools you would need to do this (usually adjustable pipe and crescent wrenches).

What to do When You are Told to Evacuate

Listen to a battery-powered radio and follow local instructions. If the danger is a chemical release and you are instructed to evacuate immediately, gather your household members and go. Take one car per household when evacuating. This will keep your household together and reduce traffic congestion and delay. In other cases, you may have time to follow these steps:

- Gather water, food, clothing, emergency supplies, and insurance and financial records.
- Wear sturdy shoes and clothing that provides some protection, such as long pants, long-sleeved shirts, and a cap.
- Secure your home. Close and lock doors and windows. Unplug appliances. If a hard freeze is likely during your absence, take actions needed to prevent damage to water pipes by freezing weather, such as:
  - Turn off the water main
  - Drain faucets
  - Turn off inside valves for external faucets and opening the outside faucets to drain
- Turn off the main water valve and electricity, if instructed to do so.
- Let others know where you are going.
- Leave early enough to avoid being trapped by severe weather.

- Follow recommended evacuation routes. Do not take shortcuts. They may be blocked. Be alert for washed-out roads and bridges. Do not drive into flooded areas. Stay away from downed power lines.

Disaster situations can be intense, stressful, and confusing. Should an evacuation be necessary, local authorities will do their best to notify the public, but do not depend entirely on this. Often, a disaster can strike with little or no warning, providing local authorities scant time to issue an evacuation order.

Also, it is possible that you may not hear of an evacuation order due to communications or power failure or not listening to your battery-powered radio. Local authorities and meteorologists could also make mistakes, including underestimating an emergency or disaster situation. In the absence of evacuation instructions from local authorities, you should evacuate if you feel you and your household are threatened or endangered. Use pre-designated evacuation routes and let others know what you are doing and your destination.

Shelter

Taking shelter is often a critical element in protecting yourself and your household in times of disaster. Sheltering can take several forms. In-place sheltering is appropriate when conditions require that you seek protection in your home, place of employment, or other location where you are located when disaster strikes. In-place sheltering may either be short-term, such as going to a safe room for a fairly short period while a tornado warning is in effect or while a chemical cloud passes. It may also be longer-term, such as when you stay in your home for several days without electricity or water services following a winter storm. We also use the term "shelter" for Mass Care facilities that provide a place to stay along with food and water for people who evacuate following a disaster.

The appropriate steps to take in preparing for and implementing short-term in-place sheltering depend entirely on the emergency situation. For instance, during a tornado warning you should go to an underground room, if such a room is available. During a chemical release, on the other hand, you should seek shelter in a room above ground level.

Long-term In-place Sheltering

Sometimes disasters make it unsafe for people to leave their residence for extended periods. Winter storms, floods, and landslides may isolate individual households and make it necessary for each household to take care of its own needs until the disaster abates, such as when snows melt and temperatures rise, or until rescue workers arrive. Your household should be prepared to be self-sufficient for three days when cut off from utilities and from outside supplies of food and water.

1. Stay in your shelter until local authorities say it's OK to leave. The length of your stay can range from a few hours to two weeks.

2. Maintain a 24-hour communications and safety watch. Take turns listening for radio broadcasts. Watch for fires.

3. Assemble an emergency toilet, if necessary.

- Use a garbage container, pail or bucket with a snug-fitting cover. If the container is small, use a larger container with a cover for waste disposal. Line both containers with plastic bags.
- After each use, pour or sprinkle a small amount of regular household disinfectant, such as chlorine bleach, into the container to reduce odors and germs.

Managing Water Supplies

Water is critical for survival. Plan to have about one gallon of water per person per day for drinking, cooking and personal hygiene. You may need more for medical emergencies.

1. Allow people to drink according to their need. The average person should drink between two and two-and-one-half quarts of water or other liquids per day, but many people need more. This will depend on age, physical activity, physical condition and time of year.

2. Never ration water unless ordered to do so by authorities. Drink the amount you need today and try to find more for tomorrow. Under no

circumstances should a person drink less than one quart of water each day. You can minimize the amount of water your body needs by reducing activity and staying cool.

3. Drink water that you know is not contaminated first. If necessary, suspicious water, such as cloudy water from regular faucets or muddy water from streams or ponds, can be used after it has been treated. If water treatment is not possible, put off drinking suspicious water as long as possible, but do not become dehydrated.

4. In addition to stored water, other sources include:

- Melted ice cubes
- Water drained from the water heater faucet, if the water heater has not been damaged
- Water dipped from the flush tanks (not the bowls) of home toilets (Bowl water can be used for pets.)
- Liquids from canned goods, such as fruit and vegetable juices

5. Carbonated beverages do not meet drinking-water requirements. Drinks containing caffeine and alcohol dehydrate the body, which increases the need for drinking water.

6. If water pipes are damaged or if local authorities advise you, turn off the main water valves to prevent water from draining away in case the water main breaks.

- The pipes will be full of water when the main valve is closed.
- To use this water, turn on the faucet at the highest point in your house (which lets air into the system).
- Then draw water, as needed, from the lowest point in your house, either a faucet or the hot water tank.

7. Unsafe water sources include:

- Radiators
- Hot water boilers (home heating system)

- Water beds (fungicides added to the water or chemicals in the vinyl may make water unsafe to use)
- Swimming pools and spas (chemicals used in them to kill germs are too concentrated for safe drinking, but can be used for personal hygiene, cleaning and related uses)

Water Treatment

Treat all water of uncertain purity before using it for drinking, food washing or preparation, washing dishes, brushing teeth or making ice. In addition to having a bad odor and taste, contaminated water can contain microorganisms that cause diseases, such as dysentery, cholera, typhoid and hepatitis.

There are many ways to treat water. None is perfect. Often the best solution is a combination of methods. Before treating, let any suspended particles settle to the bottom, or strain them through layers of clean cloth. Following are four treatment methods. The first three methods – boiling, chlorination and water treatment tablets – will kill microbes but will not remove other contaminants, such as heavy metals, salts, most other chemicals and radioactive fallout. The final method – distillation – will remove microbes, as well as most other contaminants, including radioactive fallout. Boiling is the safest method of treating water.

- Boiling water kills harmful bacteria and parasites. Bringing water to a rolling boil for one minute will kill most organisms. Let the water cool before drinking.
- Boiled water will taste better if you put oxygen back into it by pouring it back and forth between two containers. This will also improve the taste of stored water. Chlorination uses liquid chlorine bleach to kill microorganisms, such as bacteria.
- • Use regular household liquid bleach that contains no soap or scent. Some containers warn, "Not For Personal Use." You can disregard these warnings if the label states sodium hypochlorite as the only active ingredient and if you use only the small quantities mentioned in these instructions.

- Add 16 drops of unscented bleach per gallon of water stir and let stand for 30 minutes. If the water does not taste and smell of chlorine at that point, add another dose and let stand for another 15 minutes. This treatment will not kill parasitic organisms.
- If you do not have a dropper, use a spoon and a square-ended strip of paper or thin cloth about a 1/4 inch by 2 inches. Put the strip in the spoon with an end hanging down about a 1/2 inch below the scoop of the spoon. Place bleach in the spoon and carefully tip it. Drops the size of those from a medicine dropper will drip off the end of the strip.

Water treatment "purification" tablets release chlorine or iodine. They are inexpensive and available at most sporting goods stores and some drugstores. Follow the package directions carefully. NOTE: People with hidden or chronic liver or kidney disease may be adversely affected by iodized tablets and may experience worsened health problems as a result of ingestion. Iodized tablets are safe for healthy, physically fit adults and should be used only if you lack the supplies for boiling, chlorination and distillation.

Distillation involves boiling water and collecting the vapor that condenses back to water. The condensed vapor may include salt or other impurities.

- Fill a pot halfway with water.
- Tie a cup to the handle on the pot's lid, so that the cup hangs right-side up when the lid is upside-down (make sure the cup is not dangling into the water).
- Boil for 20 minutes. The water that drips from the lid into the cup is distilled.

Managing Food Supplies

1. It is important to be sanitary when storing, handling and eating food:
    - Keep food in covered containers.

- Keep cooking and eating utensils clean.
- Keep garbage in closed containers and dispose outside. Bury garbage, if necessary. Avoid letting garbage accumulate inside, both for fire and sanitation reasons.
- Keep hands clean. Wash frequently with soap and water that has been boiled or disinfected. Be sure to wash:
  - Before preparing or eating food
  - After toilet use
  - After participating in flood cleanup activities
  - After handling articles contaminated with floodwater or sewage

2. Carefully ration food for everyone except children and pregnant women. Most people can remain relatively healthy with about half as much food as usual and can survive without any food for several days.

3. Try to avoid foods high in fat and protein, since they will make you thirsty. Try to eat salt-free crackers, whole-grain cereals and canned foods with high liquid content.

4. For emergency cooking, heat food with candle warmers, chafing dishes and fondue pots, or use a fireplace. Charcoal grills and camp stoves are for outdoor use only.

5. Commercially canned food can be eaten out of the can without warming. Before heating food in a can, remove the label, thoroughly wash the can, and then disinfect it with a solution consisting of one cup of bleach in five gallons of water, and open before heating. Re-label your cans, including expiration date, with a marker:

- Do not eat foods from cans that are swollen, dented or corroded even though the product may look OK to eat.
- Do not eat any food that looks or smells abnormal, even if the can looks normal.
- Discard any food not in a waterproof container if there is any chance that it has come into contact with contaminated floodwater.

- Food containers with screw-caps, snap-lids, crimped caps (soda pop bottles), twist caps, flip tops, snap-open, and home canned foods should be discarded if they have come into contact with floodwater because they cannot be disinfected. For infants, use only pre-prepared canned baby formula. Do not use powdered formulas with treated water.

6. Your refrigerator will keep foods cool for about four hours without power if it is left unopened. Add block or dry ice to your refrigerator if the electricity will be off longer than four hours. Thawed food usually can be eaten if it is still "refrigerator cold," or re-frozen if it still contains ice crystals. To be safe, remember, "When in doubt, throw it out." Discard any food that has been at room temperature for two hours or more, and any food that has an unusual odor, color, or texture. If you are without power for a long period:

- If friends have electricity, ask them to store your frozen foods in their freezers.
- Inquire if freezer space is available in a store, church, school, or commercial freezer that has electrical service.
- Use dry ice, if available. Twenty-five pounds of dry ice will keep a 10-cubic-foot freezer below freezing for 3-4 days. Use care when handling dry ice, and wear dry, heavy gloves to avoid injury.

Recovering from a Disaster

Here is some general advice on steps to take after disaster strikes to begin putting your home, your community, and your life back to normal.

Health and Safety
Your first concern after a disaster is your household's health and safety.
1. Be aware of new hazards created by the disaster. Watch for washed-out roads, contaminated buildings, contaminated water, gas leaks, broken glass, damaged wires and slippery floors.
2. Be aware of exhaustion. Don't try to do too much at once. Set priorities and pace yourself.
3. Drink plenty of clean water. Eat well and get enough rest.

4. Wear sturdy work boots and gloves. Wash your hands thoroughly and often with soap and clean water when working in debris.

5. Inform local authorities about health and safety hazards, including chemical releases, downed power lines, washed out roads, smoldering insulation or dead animals.

Returning to a Damaged Home
Returning to a damaged home can be both physically and mentally challenging. Above all, use caution.

1. Keep a battery-powered radio with you so you can listen for emergency updates.
2. Wear sturdy work boots and gloves.
3. Before going inside, walk carefully around the outside of your home and check for loose power lines, gas leaks and structural damage. If you smell gas, do not enter the home and leave immediately. Do not enter if floodwaters remain around the building. If you have any doubts about safety, have your home inspected by a professional before entering.
4. If your home was damaged by fire, do not enter until authorities say it is safe.
5. Check for cracks in the roof, foundation and chimneys. If it looks like the building may collapse, leave immediately.
6. A battery-powered flashlight is the best source of light for inspecting a damaged home.
CAUTION: The flashlight should be turned on outside before entering a damaged home – the battery may produce a spark that could ignite leaking gas, if present.
7. Do not use oil, gas lanterns, candles or flashlights for lighting inside a damaged home. Leaking gas or other flammable materials may be present. Do not smoke. Do not turn on the lights until you're sure they're safe to use.
8. Enter the home carefully and check for damage. Be aware of loose boards and slippery floors.
9. Watch out for animals, especially poisonous snakes. Use a stick to poke through debris.
10. If you smell gas or hear a hissing or blowing sound, open a window and leave immediately. Turn off the main gas valve from the outside, if you can. Call the gas company from a neighbor's residence. If you shut off the gas supply at the main valve, you will need a professional to turn it back on.
11. Check the electrical system where visible and accessible. If you see sparks, broken or frayed wires, or if you smell hot insulation, turn off the electricity at the main fuse box or circuit breaker. If, however, you are wet,

standing in water or unsure of your safety, do not touch anything electrical. Instead, leave the building and call for help.
12. Check appliances. If appliances are wet, turn off the electricity at the main fuse box or circuit breaker. Then unplug appliances and let them dry out. Have appliances checked by a professional before using them again. Also have the electrical system checked by an electrician before turning the power back on.
13. Check the water and sewage systems. If pipes are damaged, turn off the main water valve.
14. Clean up spilled medicines, bleaches and gasoline. Open cabinets carefully. Be aware of objects that may fall.
15. Try to protect your home from further damage. Open windows and doors to get air moving through.
16. Clean and disinfect everything that got wet. Mud left behind by floodwaters can contain sewage and chemicals.
17. If your basement has flooded, pump it out gradually (about one third of the water per day) to avoid damage. The walls may collapse and the floor may buckle if the basement is pumped out while the surrounding ground is still waterlogged.
18. Check with local authorities before using any water; it could be contaminated. Wells should be pumped out and the water tested by authorities before drinking.
19. Throw out fresh food, cosmetics, and medicines that have come into contact with floodwaters.
20. Check refrigerated food for spoilage – your power supply may have been disrupted during the emergency. Throw out all spoiled food and any food that you suspect might be spoiled.
21. Call your insurance agent. Take pictures of damage. Keep good records of repair and cleaning costs.

Getting Disaster Assistance
Throughout the recovery period, it's important to monitor local radio or television reports and other media sources for information about where to get emergency housing, food, first aid, clothing and financial assistance. Following is general information about the kinds of assistance that may be available.

Direct assistance to individuals and families may come from any number of organizations. The American Red Cross is often stationed right at the scene to help people with their most immediate medical, food and housing needs.

Other voluntary organizations, such as the Salvation Army, may also provide food, shelter and supplies, and assist in cleanup efforts. Church groups and synagogues are often involved as well. In addition, social service agencies from local or state governments may be available to help people in shelters or provide direct assistance to families.

In the most severe disasters, the federal government is also called in to help individuals and families with temporary housing, counseling (for post-disaster trauma), low-interest loans and grants, and other assistance.

Small businesses and farmers are also eligible. Most federal assistance becomes available when the president of the U.S. declares a "Major Disaster" for the affected area at the request of a state governor. When this happens, FEMA may establish a Disaster Recovery Center (DRC). A DRC is a facility established in, or near to, the community affected by the disaster, where people can meet face-to-face with represented federal, state, local, and volunteer agencies to:

- Discuss their disaster-related needs
- Obtain information about disaster assistance programs
- Teleregister for assistance
- Update registration information
- Learn about measures for rebuilding that can eliminate or reduce the risk of future loss
- Learn how to complete the Small Business Administration (SBA) loan application, which is also the form used to qualify all individuals for low-cost loans or grants, including those for repair or replacement of damaged homes and furnishings
- Request the status of their Disaster Housing Application

People can apply for assistance by telephone without going to a DRC by dialing 1-800-621-FEMA (3362).

Mental Health and Crisis Counseling
The emotional toll that a disaster brings can sometimes be even more devastating than the financial strains of damage and loss of home, business or personal property. Children and the elderly are special concerns in the aftermath of disasters. Even individuals who experience a disaster "second hand" through exposure to extensive media coverage can be affected.

Crisis counseling programs often include community outreach, consultation, and education. FEMA and the state and local governments of the affected area may provide crisis-counseling assistance to help people cope with and recover from disaster. If you feel you need assistance, get help.

Coping with Disasters
You need to be aware of signs that you need help in coping with the stress of a disaster.
1. Things to remember when trying to understand disaster events:
    - No one who sees a disaster is untouched by it.
    - It is normal to feel anxious about your own safety and that of your family and close friends.
    - Profound sadness, grief and anger are normal reactions to an abnormal event.
    - Acknowledging your feelings helps you recover.
    - Focusing on your strengths and abilities will help you to heal.
    - Accepting help from community programs and resources is healthy.
    - We each have different needs and different ways of coping.
    - It is common to want to strike back at people who have caused great pain, but nothing good is accomplished by hateful language or actions.

2. Signs that adults need crisis-counseling/stress-management assistance:
    - Difficulty communicating thoughts
    - Difficulty sleeping
    - Difficulty maintaining balance
    - Easily frustrated
    - Increased use of drugs/alcohol
    - Limited attention span
    - Poor work performance
    - Headaches/stomach problems
    - Tunnel vision/muffled hearing
    - Colds or flu-like symptoms
    - Disorientation or confusion
    - Difficulty concentrating
    - Reluctance to leave home
    - Depression, sadness
    - Feelings of hopelessness
    - Mood-swings and crying easily

- Overwhelming guilt and self-doubt
- Fear of crowds, strangers, or being alone.

3. Ways to ease disaster-related stress:
    - Talk with someone about your feelings – anger, sorrow, and other emotions – even though it may be difficult.
    - Seek help from professional counselors who deal with post-disaster stress.
    - Don't hold yourself responsible for the disastrous event or be frustrated because you feel that you cannot help directly in the rescue work.
    - Take steps to promote your own physical and emotional healing by staying active in your daily life patterns or by adjusting them. This healthy outlook will help you and your household (e.g., healthy eating, rest, exercise, relaxation, meditation).
    - Maintain a normal household and daily routine, limiting demanding responsibilities of yourself and your household.
    - Spend time with family and friends.
    - Participate in memorials, rituals, and use of symbols as a way to express feelings.
    - Use existing support groups of family, friends and church.
    - Establish a family emergency plan. Feeling there is something you can do, can be very comforting.

Helping Children Cope With a Disaster

Disasters can leave children feeling frightened, confused and insecure. Whether a child has personally experienced trauma, has merely seen the event on television or heard it discussed by adults, it is important for parents and teachers to be informed and ready to help if reactions to stress begin to occur.

Children respond to trauma in many different ways. Some may have reactions very soon after the event; others may seem to be doing fine for weeks or months and then begin to show worrisome behavior. Knowing the signs that are common at different ages can help parents and teachers recognize problems and respond appropriately.

Reassurance is the key to helping children through a traumatic time. Very young children need a lot of cuddling, as well as verbal support. Answer questions about the disaster honestly, but don't dwell on frightening details or allow the subject to dominate family or classroom time indefinitely. Encourage children of all ages to express emotions through conversation, drawing or painting and to find a way to help others who were affected by the disaster. Also, limit the amount of disaster-related material (television, etc.) your children are seeing or hearing and pay careful attention to how graphic it is. Try to maintain a normal household or classroom routine and encourage children to participate in recreational activity. Reduce your expectations temporarily about performance in school or at home, perhaps by substituting less-demanding responsibilities for normal chores.

Additional information about how to communicate with children can be found on the FEMA for Kids website at www.fema.gov/kids.

Helping Others
The compassion and generosity of the American people is never more evident than after a disaster. People want to help. Here are some general guidelines on helping others after a disaster.
 1. In addition to the people you care for on a day-to-day basis, consider the needs of your neighbors and people with special needs.
 2. If you want to volunteer, check with local organizations or listen to local news reports for information about where volunteers are needed. Until volunteers are specifically requested, stay away from disaster areas.
 3. If you are needed in a disaster area, bring your own food, water and emergency supplies. This is especially important in cases where a large area has been affected and emergency items are in short supply.
 4. Do not drop off food, clothing or any other item to a government agency or disaster relief organization unless a particular item has been requested. Normally these organizations do not have the resources to sort through the donated items.
 5. You can give a check or money order to a recognized disaster relief organization.
 6. If your company wants to donate emergency supplies, donate a quantity of a given item or class of items (such as nonperishable food) rather than a mix of different items. Also, determine where your donation is going, how it's going to get there, who is going to unload it and how it's going to be distributed. Without sufficient planning, much needed supplies will be left unused.

Chapter Fifteen. Travel Safe

Given the heightened threat of terrorism, security is now tighter in the air, on the railroads and on the highways, and travelers, more than ever, need to keep their eyes open and be aware of what is going on around them.

Do Your Homework

Before heading on a trip, especially overseas, check for travel warnings, weather forecasts and advisories. Get a map and make sure you know where you are going. If you are going to be on the road for a few days, make sure you have accommodations booked in advance. You don't want to be driving around strange areas late at night trying to find a room.

If you are traveling overseas, visit the State Department's website. It issues travel advisories and updates these regularly. You can find them on its website **www.state.gov**, call the State Department's information line at 888-407-4747 for the information or dial 202-647-3000 on your fax machine and follow the prompts to get it faxed to you. The department can also supply you with information sheets on individual countries, which include such helpful information as whether a wide array of pharmaceuticals is generally available in shops. If you are traveling overseas, see our special section at the back of this book.

Medications - Bring Extra Meds

In case your return home is delayed for whatever reason, bring medications for an extra couple of days with you. But handle them with care. Inspectors at border crossings, airports, and the like are checking more bags more carefully, so it's a good idea to keep medications in their original packages.

Airlines have banned passengers from carrying a variety of everyday items, including metal nail files and corkscrews. If you're planning to fly and need to carry needles for medical reasons, you'll need to bring the corresponding medication, with original labeling, with you, says the Federal Aviation

Administration (FAA). Since the prescription label is on the outside of boxes of insulin vials, the FAA suggests that passengers with diabetes bring their insulin in this box.

Diabetics can carry on board lancets, as long as they're capped, and can also bring accompanying glucose meters with the manufacturer's name embossed on the meters. For links to more information see **www.diabetes.org**. Since individual airlines may have additional requirements for passengers carrying these medical devices, call yours in advance for details.

A Month Before You Leave

Get Immunized Early

Buy your guidebook and check the Centers for Disease Control and Prevention's destination-specific lists of recommended vaccinations and health precautions. You may need to get some immunizations at least a month before departing.

Get a Checkup

See your primary care physician for vaccinations and a physical to make sure you are OK to travel. If you'll be crossing time zones, ask your doctor whether you should continue taking your meds at your regular, home-zone time, or switch – and how. Ask if any foods you're likely to encounter while away might interact with your meds. Leafy greens, for example, can decrease the effects of some blood-thinning drugs. Get two letters from your doctor if you're crossing international borders. The first should explain any medical problems you have, and their treatment. It'll come in handy if you need to consult with health care providers while away. You'll also need one that lists prescription meds (including their generic names) and any alternative remedies you take, as well as why, when, how (whether you use a syringe, for instance), and at what dosage. The letter should note that the quantity you're packing is appropriate for your needs, because every country has its own rules about bringing prescription drugs across its borders. For instance,

Valium and similar drugs are prohibited in Mexico. Having all the proper documentation will ease your way through customs and help you get replacement meds should you lose yours en route.

Consider Traveler's Insurance

Call your health insurance company before leaving to find out exactly what's covered when you are traveling abroad. Many policies don't cover evacuation or non-emergency care abroad, so ask.

Packing

Get Your Numbers Straight

Program your doctor's contact information into your cell phone, or jot it in your address book.

Keep Your Meds in Their Original Containers

This goes for all medicines: prescription, over-the-counter, and alternative. If you need a syringe, make sure it's in a clearly labeled container, too. You'll make life easier for security staff at airports and border crossings.

Carry Must-take Meds On Board

If you're flying, put prescription drugs, and any syringes you might need, in your carry-on bag, together with the letter from your doctor, so they're accessible and safe. Storage conditions in cargo holds can affect the stability of certain meds, but you should never put medicines in checked luggage, which may or may not arrive at the same destination.

Remember Your Paperwork

Make a copy of those prescriptions and letters from your doctor; then put one set in your carry-on bag and another in a suitcase. If one gets lost or stolen, you'll have a backup.

Traveling by Car

There are more than 230-million registered motor vehicles in the U.S. and almost 200-million licensed drivers, and every year they travel 2,890,893,000,000 miles on our roads. It is not surprising, therefore, that every year more than 42,000 people are killed and more than 2.8 million injured in traffic accidents. In addition, there are more than 4.3-million property-damage-only traffic accidents.

Safe Driving Tips

If someone else is in the car, you should refrain from talking with your hands, and realize that you are doing something that could, in one instant, become life threatening. When speaking with others in your car don't feel as if you need to look at them when carrying on a conversation. Keep your eyes on the road. ALWAYS PAY ATTENTION TO THE ROADWAY.

Remember that cell phones and all other distractions increase your chances of having an accident. If you must use your cell phone on a regular basis while driving consider reducing your risk by purchasing a miniature headset or hands-free device at your local electronics store.

The left lane of any interstate highway is for passing. Staying out of the left lane (and in one of the right lanes) when not passing greatly reduces social stress on the highways, which makes them safer for everyone.

Always remember to buckle your seatbelt – even if the ride is just around the corner.

Keep your children in proper restraint seats, or properly adjusted safety belts if they are older. (Using the phrase "OK everybody ... buckle up!" works well before starting the car.) Keep your rear-view, and side mirrors adjusted for maximum visibility.

If you wish to be seen more easily in daily traffic, consider using your headlights during the daytime as well as at night, and always remember to use your headlights when traveling on two-lane highways regardless of the time of day.

Overtaking Tips

Always pass trucks and buses quickly. When you are approaching these vehicles from the rear, always judge your passing speed and don't begin the passing process only to find yourself stuck behind another vehicle ... trapped beside the truck or bus. Always wait to let the vehicle in front of you complete their pass before beginning yours.

Be aware that most large commercial vehicles these days have 500 horsepower or more, and are equipped with cruise control. Yet their companies have limited their top speed through their engines' computer system to ensure safe driving and better insurance rates. If you notice one of these vehicles creeping up on you, then make a decision to speed up and pull away, or slow down and let it pass.

Trucks and buses try to maintain a safe distance between themselves and the vehicle in front of them. Yet many automobile drivers commonly invade this "Safety Zone" to increase their position on the road. When passing a truck or bus, always leave at least 50 feet (or five car lengths) of space between you and the other vehicle before merging back into the lane in front. Never zoom around a truck or bus only to pull directly in front of it. Drivers who do this have no control over what might happen in front of them ... placing their lives at risk, as well as the lives of others. The larger vehicle will never be able to stop in time should the car driver need to hit the brakes.

Remember that If you can't see a truck's rear-view mirrors, then the driver cannot see you. Let this simple fact be a gauge as to how close behind it you should be. Always stay back far enough so that you can see the mirrors.

Bad Weather Driving Tips

Snow and Ice

Bridges and overpasses freeze first. Slow down and avoid sudden changes in speed or direction. Keep windows clear of snow and ice. Keep your speed steady and slow, but not too slow. In deeper snow, it's often necessary to use the car's momentum to keep moving. Use brakes very cautiously. Abrupt braking can cause brake lock-up, which causes you to lose steering control.

Antilock brakes are designed to overcome a loss of steering control on wet or slippery roads. Yet they have little or no effect on ice. To make antilock brakes work correctly, or work at all, you should apply constant, firm pressure to the pedal. During an emergency stop, push the brake pedal all the way to the floor. If you get stuck in snow, straighten the wheels and accelerate slowly. Avoid spinning the tires, because the heat friction caused by spinning tires melts the snow and creates a thin layer of ice. Use sand or cinders under the drive wheels to increase traction if you get a little stuck. Never stand in traffic to push a car that's stuck. Someone else could lose control and seriously injure or even kill you.

High Winds

Use extra care and consider whether a trailer, van or other "high-profile" vehicle should be operated at all.

Rain

The road becomes slippery as water mixes with road oils, grease and dirt. Also, your car's tires tend to ride on the surface water, reducing traction ... Slow down.

Visibility is often impaired. Turn on your headlights at the first sign of rain. Use the defroster or air conditioner to keep windows and mirrors clear.

Fog

Stay to the right of the roadway. Turn on your headlights – day or night – to low beam. If fog thickens, run your hazard flashers to aid others coming up from behind you, increasing the ability for others to see you better. If you're having difficulty seeing the road's edge, pull off at the next exit, well out of the traffic lane, turn on the emergency flashers and leave your headlights on, and your vehicle running.

Severe Weather

Severe hailstorms – find shelter by driving under an overpass or bridge.

Severe thunderstorms – listen to your car radio and stay alert.

If you spot a tornado, don't try to outrun it. Get out of the car; find shelter in a ditch or low-lying area and lie face down to protect yourself from flying debris.

Hurricanes – avoid low areas and move inland while there's still plenty of time.

Cell Phones and Other Distractions

Distracted driving – including the use of cell phones -- is a major contributor to automobile crashes. Between 4,000 and 8,000 crashes related to distracted driving occur daily in the United States. In a year, they contribute to as many as one-half of the 7 million U.S. crashes reported annually.

How do hand-held cell phones factor into the equation? Using a cell phone while driving can increase your chances of being involved in a crash. However, cell phones aren't the only problem. Other distractions, such as looking at outside objects and other people in the vehicle, pose a greater risk of contributing to crashes than cell phone use.

Why are hand-held cell phones at the heart of the debate? Hand-held cell phones are readily visible to other drivers. When people chance upon a distracted driver and notice a cell phone, they naturally blame the phone. Most drivers are frustrated when they see inconsiderate, inattentive drivers talking on cell phones. It's often more difficult to determine if a distracted driver is talking to a passenger, tuning the radio or eating.

What about hands-free phones? Hands-free phones are not risk-free. The hands-free feature is simply a convenience: It does not increase safety. Studies show that hands-free cellular phones distract drivers the same as hand-held phones, because it is the conversation that distracts the driver — not the device.

Will banning hand-held cell phones improve safety? Not according to current research. A study funded by the AAA Foundation for Traffic Safety about the effects of cell phone use on driver attention found that the distraction of using a hands-free cell phone and tuning a radio is similar. Regarding the question of banning specific devices, such as hand-held cell phones, two facts are clear: Banning hand-held phones, but allowing hands-free phones is likely to have little or no effect on safety. No studies show hands-free phones offer safety advantages over hand-held phones. The distracting factor is the conversation — not the device itself. And no one can legislate when and what drivers think.

The bottom line – Drivers need to keep their eyes on the road and their minds on driving. AAA recommends drivers not use their cell phones while driving. However, if using a phone is essential, drivers should follow these safety tips:

TIPS FOR SAFE CELL PHONE USE WHILE DRIVING

- Recognize that driving requires your full attention.
- Before you get behind the wheel, familiarize yourself with the features of your cell phone.
- Use your cell phone only if it is absolutely necessary.
- If you must use your phone, do so at a safe time and place.
- Ask a passenger in the car to place the call for you and, if possible, speak in your place.
- Plan your conversation in advance and keep it short.
- Inform the person you're calling that you are speaking from the car.
- Hang the phone up as soon as possible, especially in heavy traffic and hazardous weather conditions.
- Secure your phone in the car, so that it doesn't become a projectile in a crash.

Road Rage

No matter how safe a driver you are, it is the actions of others that you have to be concerned about. One of the most worrying new trends is road rage, which in many cases has led to fatalities.

The aggressive driver has become a menace on our highways to the degree that our lawmakers are involved in trying to find ways to stop the aggressive driver from physically harming others.

It is estimated that about one-third of crashes and two-thirds of the resulting fatalities can be attributed to behavior associated with aggressive driving. For years the highway safety spotlight has been on the impaired driver, the speeding driver, and the unbelted driver. However, today we must add the aggressive driver to the list of major highway-accident producers.

So, who is an aggressive driver? An aggressive driver is anybody whose driving behavior is characterized by impatience and a lack of concern for others. This behavior endangers both people and property. This definition includes a diverse range of driving behaviors, from erratic or abnormal maneuvers to dueling or violence on the road.

Aggressive drivers tend to do the following: Speed, tailgate, fail to yield, weave in and out of traffic, pass on the right, make quick and unsafe lane changes, run stop signs and lights, make rude hand and facial gestures, scream, honk, and flash their car's headlights. Aggressive drivers behave in this manner because they feel safe and powerful behind the wheel of a big, heavy machine, and they allow their high frustration level to diminish any concern they should have for others.

Driving Tips

- Don't retaliate. Never take the other driver's behavior personally. He/she is only reacting on a road-rage instinct.
- Don't make eye contact with an angry driver.
- Before you react to anything that is done to you, please ask yourself, "Is getting back at that jerk worth my life?"
- Be polite and courteous, even when others are not.
- Always ask yourself: "Could the other driver have possibly made a mistake?"
- If you are harassed by another driver and being followed, do not go home. Go to the nearest police station.
- Slow down and relax!
- Never underestimate other drivers' capacity for mayhem.
- Reduce your driving stress by allowing enough time to get where you are going. Know the roads that are under construction and listen to weather reports that may cause traffic delays. Practice patience and keep your cool.

- Remember that you cannot control the drivers around you, but you can control the way they affect you.

Much of the time, the damaging behavior continues after the aggressive driver has gotten out of his vehicle. Aggressive drivers use a variety of weapons, such as their fists and feet, tire irons and jack handles, baseball bats, knives, razor blades and defensive sprays, such as mace, and guns. If you are involved in an incident with an aggressive driver, stay calm and do not provoke him or her. Wait patiently for the police to arrive.

Subway and Bus Security

As a general precaution, whether you're in the subway, the bus, or even in the street, appear confident. Always look as if you know where you're going, and you're better off not displaying money in public. If you're alert and aware, you can make your subway and bus trips even more secure.

Off-Hours Waiting Areas

Avoid standing at the end of subway platforms or on an empty platform. Instead, wait in the Off-Hours Waiting Area, particularly at night. Many stations have one, generally located near a station booth. Speak to the station agent or other Transit employees if you have a problem. Use a talkback box (mounted on a platform column) to get help in a station where you're not visible to the station agent. When you speak into the box, the agent can speak with you. You can also use a public phone to dial 911 (the police) if you need help. This call is free. Electronic signs in many Off-Hours Waiting Areas indicate when a train is approaching the station. If you wait near the sign, you will have enough time to walk to the platform as the train arrives.

Protect Yourself Against Pickpockets

Stay awake. A pickpocket's easiest victim is a sleeping passenger. If you feel drowsy, it's best to get up and stand, or take another seat. When you find yourself alone in an empty subway car, move to a car that has a conductor (usually in the center of the train), a train operator (front car), or other riders.

Being alert and staying in a subway car with other people are always good precautions. Although pickpockets often target people who are alone and asleep, they know how to operate in crowds as well. That's why you should be wary of being pushed or bumped. But even when there aren't many people around you on a bus or in the subway, never keep your wallet or money in a back pocket, and keep all bags, backpacks, and pocketbooks securely closed. Overlooking these things can make you an easy target.

Keep alert if you see or hear a commotion. It could be a pickpocket's trick to divert your attention. And, speaking of remaining alert, be extra cautious if you use a headset. They tend to reduce your awareness. If your pocket is picked while you're on a bus, call out to the bus operator immediately. He or she can request police assistance.

How to Avoid Bag or Chain Snatching

Bag and chain snatchers are more obvious than pickpockets, but the result is the same. Following a few precautions can better protect your valuables. Purse snatching is a crime of opportunity. You can eliminate that opportunity. Every female carrying a purse is a potential target. Senior citizens are especially susceptible to these criminals, since they may not be readily able to defend themselves and pursue their assailants. Purse snatching is a crime that can be easily prevented when you take away the opportunity from the thief. Most purse snatchers are juveniles under the age of 18, who are waiting for the next opportunity.

WHAT YOU CAN DO

- When you hide the "prize," you protect yourself.
- Shop with a friend, travel together – you're always safer in company.
- If you are in a high-crime area, have only three or four small bills placed inside your purse. Credit cards, currency, driver's license, keys and jewelry should be carried in a coat or sweater pocket, or concealed on your person to reduce the opportunity of large losses.
- If you carry a purse, don't wrap the strap around your shoulder, neck or wrist. If your purse is grabbed, a strong strap will not yield easily and you may be injured.
- Never carry anything more valuable than you can afford to lose.

- Always leave all unnecessary credit cards at home.
- When you shop and carry a purse, place it in your shopping bag.
- Never leave your purse on a store counter or in a shopping cart, even for a moment.

DON'T CARRY WEAPONS THAT CAN BE USED AGAINST YOU

You should carry a police whistle and a small flashlight on your key chain where they're readily available. Make it a habit to carry your key chain in a pocket, NOT in your purse. Never put your name and address on your house keys or car keys. This is a simple way of telling the thief who you are and where you live.

CALL THE POLICE IMMEDIATELY

Most victims are attacked from behind. They don't get a good look at their attacker. And when a juvenile gets away with it once, he or she will try it again. If attacked, call the police immediately. Try to remember all details – help the police help you.

Subway Safety

Most subway accidents result from slips, trips, and falls on stairways when someone is in a rush. The best safety advice we can give you is: slow down when you are on the stairs, and hold the handrail.

On Platforms

Some trains are shorter (have fewer cars) when it's not rush hour because there are fewer passengers using the subway. Some short trains operate without a conductor. On those trains, the train operator opens and closes the doors, makes station announcements, and assists customers, if needed. Consider waiting at the center of the platform at these times. At most stations, there are signs that read: During Off-Hours, Trains Stop Here. If you stand near the center of the platform near the sign, you won't have to rush when the train arrives. While you're waiting, please stand behind the yellow protective strip, away from the platform edge. No matter what situation arises, keep off the tracks. Tracks contain 600 volts of live electricity. If you drop something on the tracks, go to the station booth and tell the agent.

In Subway Cars

Boarding between subway cars may seem like a time-saver, but it is highly dangerous. It's also dangerous to try to keep subway doors from closing when you are entering or exiting the train. They are not like elevator doors and will not reopen automatically. In addition, make sure that pocketbooks, knapsacks, clothing, packages, umbrellas, and other personal items are clear of the closing doors. When you're inside a moving train, never ride between cars or lean against doors. When you are standing, always hold on.

Using the Emergency Cord

Use the emergency cord only to prevent an accident or injury. For example, if someone gets caught between closing subway-car doors and is being dragged, pull the cord. But if your train is between stations and someone aboard becomes ill, do not pull the emergency cord. The train will stop, preventing medical professionals from reaching the sick passenger. A sick person is better off if the train goes to the nearest station where police and medical services will be waiting, or can be quickly summoned, without interruption.

On Escalators

Never run or walk on escalators; always hold the handrail and face forward. If you're with a child, hold hands. It's not a good idea for small children to hold escalator handrails. Escalator steps are always moving and have spaces that can grab. This means you should avoid resting packages (or yourself) on the stairs. You'll also want to keep clothing and shoes away from the sides. In addition, make sure that laces on footwear are tied. When you leave an escalator, step off, rather than ride off.

On Elevators

Children don't know that elevator doors can hurt them. You need to keep youngsters away from them. So, either hold children's hands or, if you're using a stroller, keep children's hands inside and never use a stroller to block closing doors. Watch clothing, bags, and other personal items — they can get caught in closing doors, too.

With Baby Strollers

Fold strollers so that you can carry infants on stairs or escalators. Strap your child in snugly at all other times. When you're on the platform, keep the stroller away from the edge and apply the stroller brake. That's because platforms tilt toward the tracks to allow for drainage, and the stroller could roll onto the tracks. Never place a stroller between closing subway-car doors. Watch out for the gap between the platform's edge and train when you board. (That's always a good idea, even when you're traveling alone.) And it's better if you board in the center of the train. The conductor is usually there, making it easier to get attention in case of a problem.

Buses

Don't run for the bus – that's when most accidents happen. Slips, trips, and falls are the most common causes of injuries. If you're at the front of the bus, please stay behind the white line. Avoid standing in the stairwell (rear-door step) or leaning against the rear door. And if you're a wheelchair user, please allow the bus operator to secure your chair. While you're riding, keep your head and arms inside bus windows. When you're ready to get off, signal the bus operator two blocks before your stop so that he or she has sufficient time to stop smoothly. We also advise holding the railing when you exit the bus, especially in winter. Bus steps and sidewalks become slippery from snow. As you leave the bus, watch for cars. This is particularly important when the bus operator has not been able to pull completely into the bus stop. Also, avoid crossing in front of the bus after you get off.

Request a Stop

Bus users who travel between 10 p.m. and 5 a.m. can Request-a-Stop. Ask the bus operator to let you off anywhere along the route, even if it isn't a designated stop. The bus operator will comply as long as he or she thinks it's a safe location, and will still make all regularly scheduled stops.

Trains

The U.S. government, private industry and public agencies have all taken the responsibility of trying to secure our nation's commuter railroads and mass-transit systems very seriously. The Department of Homeland Security has been at the forefront of this initiative by coordinating a comprehensive set of security initiatives that will aid in reducing the risk of a catastrophic attack on both mass transit and/or commuter rail systems. A focused effort on information sharing between all applicable stakeholders and government agencies has allowed for the development of new security measures and plans, increased training/public awareness campaigns and security program funding assistance. The federal government will continue to provide expert guidance and assistance to transit and rail agencies as well as seeking to mitigate any potential terrorist threat, domestic or foreign, intended to cause harm or disruption to this nation's national transportation system.

General Safety Tips

Surrounding Awareness

When traveling, be on the lookout for:

- Unusual behavior and suspicious activity
- Suspicious or unattended packages, devices, baggage, suitcases
- Emergency notifications and procedures given by the station manager or train operator
- Location of emergency exits and intercoms in stations and on trains

Irregular and/or Suspicious Activities and Items

When observing, look for people who:

- Look lost and/or are wandering around
- Appear to be conducting surveillance (using cameras/video)
- Abandon an item and leave the area quickly
- Openly possess a weapon or any prohibited or dangerous item

You should be aware of items or devices that:

- Are hidden or abandoned
- Are connected to wires, timers, tanks, or bottles
- Appear to be releasing a mist, gas, vapor, or odor
- Appear to be suspicious or dangerous, such as a canister, tank, metal box, bottle, etc.

What do you do if you notice a threat?

Contact authorities: local law enforcement, security personnel, conductor, or 911. Remain calm and answer questions as best as possible. Avoid using radios and cellular telephones within 50 feet of materials or devices that may be explosives.

Onboard Safety

While onboard any Amtrak train please note the following for a safer and more enjoyable trip:

- Use seat backs and handrails while walking through the train.
- Watch your step when boarding and leaving the train.
- Watch your step moving from car to car while the train is in motion, as the vestibules can be slippery.
- Be sure to step over the gap between the train and platform.
- Leave personal food items and baggage at your seat.
- Wear shoes at all times and use caution when wearing shoes without rubber soles.
- Never attempt to board or exit a moving train.
- Make sure you familiarize yourself with the safety card found in most seat backs.

Safety at the Station

While in any Amtrak station please note the following for a safer, more enjoyable trip:

- Arrive at least 30 minutes before your train is due to depart.

- Check in early to arrange for pre-boarding if you need extra time or assistance.
- Watch your step on station stairs, escalators, and train platforms.
- Please stand back from the edge of the platform.
- Help children when boarding and leaving the train.
- Take care when crossing the gap between the train and platform.
- Use only Red Cap agents to help you with your baggage.
- Please report any suspicious behavior to police, Amtrak Police or station personnel.

Aircraft

Security awareness is everyone's responsibility. To ensure that your travel is safe, secure and efficient, take time to make security awareness an integral part of your travel experience.

General Guidelines

Be aware of suspicious activity in and around your immediate surroundings. Inform the proper authorities if you are concerned about an unattended item or suspicious activity in and around any facility. Describe the device, do not touch it and do not use a cell phone within 50 feet of a suspicious item. Be extra careful if you work on your laptop. Working takes your attention away from your surroundings. Remember to control all carry-on bags and keep your items and tickets with you at all times. Medicines, cash, jewelry, business papers and valuables should be packed in carry-on bags. Never leave anything unattended, as it could be subjected to tampering and/or theft. Never carry anything for another person, especially for someone you do not know.

Before the Airport

- Do not pack or bring prohibited items to the airport. Read the Permitted and Prohibited Items list that the airline will provide with your travel documents. Place valuables, such as jewelry, cash and laptop computers, in carry-on baggage only.
- Tape your business card to the bottom of your laptop.

- Avoid wearing clothing, jewelry and accessories that contain metal. Metal items may set off the alarm on the metal detector.
- Avoid wearing shoes that contain metal or have thick soles or heels. Many types of footwear will require additional screening even if the metal detector does not sound the alarm.
- Put all undeveloped film and cameras with film in your carry-on baggage. Checked baggage screening equipment will damage undeveloped film.
- Declare firearms and ammunition to your airline and place them in your checked baggage.
- If you wish to lock your baggage, use a TSA-recognized lock.
- Do not bring lighters or prohibited matches to the airport.
- Do not pack wrapped gifts and do not bring wrapped gifts to the checkpoint. Wrap on arrival or ship your gifts prior to your departure. TSA may have to unwrap packages for security reasons.

At the Airport

Each adult traveler needs to keep available his/her airline boarding pass and government-issued photo ID until exiting the security checkpoint. Due to different airport configurations, at many airports you will be required to display these documents more than once. Place the following items **IN** your carry-on baggage or in a plastic bag prior to entering the screening checkpoint:

- Mobile phones
- Keys
- Loose change
- Money clips
- PDAs (personal data assistants)
- Large amounts of jewelry
- Metal hair decorations
- Large belt buckles

Take your laptop and video cameras with cassettes **OUT** of their cases and place them in a bin provided at the checkpoint. Take **OFF** all outer coats, suit coats, jackets and blazers.

Clear Medical and Kids' Companions

After the 9/11 attacks, airlines began allowing only ticketed passengers – with ID – beyond screening checkpoints. If, for medical reasons, you need a companion to accompany you to your seat, or you need an escort to do the same for a child who is traveling alone, airlines will accommodate you. Call the airline in advance to find out what kind of identification that person will need, and what procedures to follow. For more information, go to www.faa.gov.

Allow Extra Time

Bring extra food and drinks, if you have special dietary needs, or just can't stomach air terminal fare. Thanks to tighter airport security and more thorough checks, passengers will need to get to the airport at least two hours before their flights are scheduled to leave.

Report Suspicious Parcels and People

Keep an eye on your bags at all times, and notify security immediately if you spot an unattended bag at the airport, train or bus station. Do the same if you see a suspicious person. If a fellow passenger is acting strangely in flight, discreetly alert the flight attendant.

Staying Safe During a Hijacking

It's not likely to happen. But should your plane be hijacked, your best bet is to follow the flight crews' instructions. All flight crewmembers have been trained in dealing with these security threats.

Stay Healthy On the Plane

Drinking

Because the air inside planes is drier than outside, your risk of dehydration is higher. Drinking alcohol will dehydrate you further. Drink water or fruit juice whenever you're even slightly thirsty. Always take your own bottle of water and ask for a glass of water each time the flight attendant offers. If she's too busy to give you a refill, you'll have your own supply.

Flex Your Muscles

Sit still for more than 2 hours, and the blood in your veins can pool and form potentially life-threatening clots. This condition is known as deep-vein thrombosis and was thought to be caused by sitting in cramped conditions in economy class. Now it is known that it is caused by lack of exercise – no matter how much you paid for your seat. Prevent the problem by flexing your muscles, moving your limbs and walking around if the "fasten seat belt" sign is off.

Travel Troubleshooting Guide

Non-emergency medical problem

- Traveling in the United States: If you belong to an HMO, call your insurer to find out if there are in-network providers in the area. If not, ask if it will waive out-of-network surcharges.
- Abroad: Contact the US Consulate, which should provide a list of English-speaking doctors. Most insurers won't cover the cost, however.

Medical Emergency

Traveling in the United States: Head straight for the ER. Your insurance should cover the cost for a true emergency. Abroad: Head straight for the nearest ER. Your insurance should cover the tab.

Lost medications

Traveling in the United States: Call your doctor and have him or her phone in a prescription to the nearest pharmacy. Some insurers cover one replacement per lost prescription.
Abroad: Contact the foreign embassy in the United States before leaving to inquire what arrangements would need to be made. Some insurers will cover; others won't.

Safe Cruising

More than 10 million people will go cruising this year and have a fabulous time. Because of heightened security, however, it will take longer to embark and disembark, so plan accordingly. Make sure you have enough time to get to the cruise terminal and complete the embarkation procedure before the ship sails! Expect and plan for longer times to park, check-in and to pass through the security checkpoints. You may experience some inconvenience and delays — please plan to leave for the airport/cruise terminal early. And be patient and understanding. Boarding will be denied without presenting proper documents. Check with your travel agent or the cruise line regarding the documentation you will require.

- U.S. Citizens — A passport or a birth certificate (original or certified copy) plus a picture is needed.
- ID card issued by a federal, state, or local government agency is required. A voter registration card or Social Security card is not considered to be proof of citizenship. Children under 16 years of age do not require a picture ID card.
- Non-U.S. Citizens — Valid passports and visas (except for waiver countries) are required, in addition to Alien Registration Cards (ARC or "Green" cards), if an individual is a Resident Alien living in the United States. Certain Canadian and Mexican citizens may travel with alternative documentation depending on their alien status in the United States.
- For customs and immigration purposes, guests are also required to have necessary visa, passport and other travel authorization documents based upon their nationality and country of residence.

For Cruise Passengers Arriving by Air

- Checking luggage at off-airport sites is prohibited. You may still use these sites to obtain boarding passes and seat assignments, but luggage will need to be checked at the airport. Some cruise lines offer airport check-in at the cruise terminal after disembarkation.
- No form of weapon will be permitted on your person or in carry-on luggage. Regardless of the size, items, such as small penknives, scissors and such, should be left at home or placed in checked baggage.
- Only ticketed passengers will be permitted through the security checkpoints. Make sure that you have acceptable photo identification.
- Travelers with e-tickets must hold one of the following documents indicating a flight departure for a current date: A boarding pass or

paper ticket, a receipt for an electronic ticket (e-ticket), or an itinerary generated by an airline or travel agency.
- Check your cruise documentation for up-to-date and appropriate air travel information to comply with security checkpoint measures.
- Check-in at the ticket counter if you are unsure about passing through security.
- Vehicles parked near the airport will be closely monitored and should not be unattended.
- DO NOT leave your luggage unattended at any time.
- You will likely notice additional uniformed, law enforcement officers and FAA canine teams patrolling the airports.

Travel Tips

- Consider purchasing trip/vacation cancellation and interruption insurance from your travel agent or cruise line.
- Review your cruise documents in advance for important information, guidelines and tips.
- Prior to leaving home, call the airline — or check their website for flight arrival/departure information.
- Be at the airport early — at least two hours unless local circumstances require more time.
- Minimize your carry-on luggage AND be prepared to have it searched. Suspicious items (knives, scissors, clippers, files, etc.) may be confiscated and subject you to a further delay.
- Make sure that your baggage is clearly tagged with your name and contact information and that you have completed and attached the cruise tags provided with your cruise documentation.
- Verify that any required medical items are with you and not in checked luggage.
- Verify that you have the proper identification required for all travelers in your party and that it is on your person — not in checked luggage.
- Expects some delays and be patient.
- Enjoy your cruise and have a great vacation.

Severe Acute Respiratory Syndrome (SARS) and Cruise Travel

Although there have been no reports of SARS on any cruise ship operating in North America to date, the membership of the ICCL has taken increased health and safety measures as a matter of caution.

Monitoring/Prevention of SARS on Cruise Ships

Individual cruise lines are closely monitoring the SARS situation around the clock, and, depending on various factors, such as their employees, passengers and ports of call, have implemented various procedures to ensure the health of everyone onboard. These steps have included:

- Screening of both passengers and crew who are arriving within 10 days from CDC identified SARS-travel-alert areas.
- Working to proactively educate both passengers and crew about SARS and its symptoms and will, as appropriate, deny boarding to any passenger that meets certain risk factors for SARS.
- Re-routing arriving passenger and vessel itineraries away from locations for which there are current travel warnings.

Enhanced Cruise Ship Procedures/Protocols

Over the past several years, ICCL member cruise lines have enhanced the safety and security of passengers and crew through the adoption of the most comprehensive and proactive health and sanitation protocols in the travel and tourism industry. Currently, all member cruise lines participate in a voluntary vessel sanitation program administered by the CDC. Cruise-industry health and sanitation protocols, developed in conjunction with the CDC, are effective in reducing the transmission of infectious illnesses aboard ships.

Should a suspected SARS case be identified on a cruise ship, all members of the ICCL have trained medical staff onboard with appropriate isolation and treatment facilities. The disinfectants available for use by ICCL member lines are believed to be the most effective agents available against the virus that is presently thought to cause SARS.

On Vacation

Water Safety

Every year, about 800 children younger than 14 die as a result of unintentional drowning in the United States; another 2,700 are treated in emergency rooms for nearly drowning. And a review by the National Safe Kids Campaign found that in nine out of 10 cases, children drowned while under supervision, with 94% of parents saying they were watching their kids. The report revealed that parents were also chatting, reading, eating, dialing the phone, having an alcoholic drink, or closing their eyes to relax.

Staying Afloat

Non-swimmers and beginners should wear a personal flotation device (PFD) approved by the US Coast Guard (USCG) when in or near the water. It should be a snug fit, based on the child's weight and age. Use a model with a crotch strap to keep it in place in the water on kids under age 10. It's not a substitute for supervision, but it could help a child keep his or her head up if he or she slips into the pool. Water wings, pool rings, and rafts are OK as toys only, meaning keep your eyes on the child who is playing with them. And don't rely on bathing suits with built-in flotation systems or non-USCG strap-on floats.

Have a Designated Water Watcher

Whenever kids swim, responsible adults or teens should take 20-minute shifts standing guard. That means no talking, eating, drinking, or playing with the kids while on duty.

Sign Kids up for Swim Class

The Red Cross recommends lessons beginning at age 4 or 5. Classes should include water safety tips. For info on water-watcher tags, swimming classes, and USCG-approved PFDs, visit the **American Red Cross**.

Traveling Overseas

If you are traveling abroad here are the top 10 tips you need to make your trip easier:

1. Make sure you have a signed, valid passport and visas, if required. Also, before you go, fill in the emergency information page of your passport!
2. Read the Consular Information Sheets (and Public Announcements or Travel Warnings, if applicable) for the countries you plan to visit.
3. Familiarize yourself with local laws and customs of the countries to which you are traveling. Remember, the U.S. Constitution does not follow you! While in a foreign country, you are subject to its laws.
4. Make two copies of your passport identification page. This will facilitate replacement if your passport is lost or stolen. Leave one copy at home with friends or relatives. Carry the other with you in a separate place from your passport.
5. Leave a copy of your itinerary with family or friends at home so that you can be contacted in case of an emergency.
6. Do not leave your luggage unattended in public areas. Do not accept packages from strangers.
7. Prior to your departure, you should register with the nearest U.S. embassy or consulate through the State Department's travel registration website. Registration will make your presence and whereabouts known in case it is necessary to contact you in an emergency. In accordance with the Privacy Act, information on your welfare and whereabouts may not be released without your express authorization. Remember to leave a detailed itinerary and the numbers or copies of your passport or other citizenship documents with a friend or relative in the United States.
8. To avoid being a target of crime, try not to wear conspicuous clothing and expensive jewelry, and do not carry excessive amounts of money or unnecessary credit cards.
9. In order to avoid violating local laws, deal only with authorized agents when you exchange money or purchase art or antiques.
10. If you get into trouble, contact the nearest U.S. embassy.

Field Notes

Field Notes

Field Notes

Edible Florida

The great outdoors provides a year-round abundant supply of free and nutritional food for those willing to explore it.

There are tender leaves that can be used in salads or cooked as greens; nuts, seeds and berries for trailside snacks and roots for vegetables for vegetables or ground to produce flour.

Foraging for food is fun and free if you want to add some interesting and nutritious ingredients to your meals or need a handy trail-side snack. In a disaster knowing what to forage could be the difference between life and death.

For centuries, wild plants and herbs have also been used to treat ailments in the countryside and some of these remedies can still be very useful today.

A Beginner's Guide to Edible Florida takes a detailed look at many of the edible, herbal and culinary plants that can found throughout southeastern U.S.

The guide has full color pictures of all the plants and describes where they are found, which parts are edible and how to prepare or use them.

Available from Amazon.com

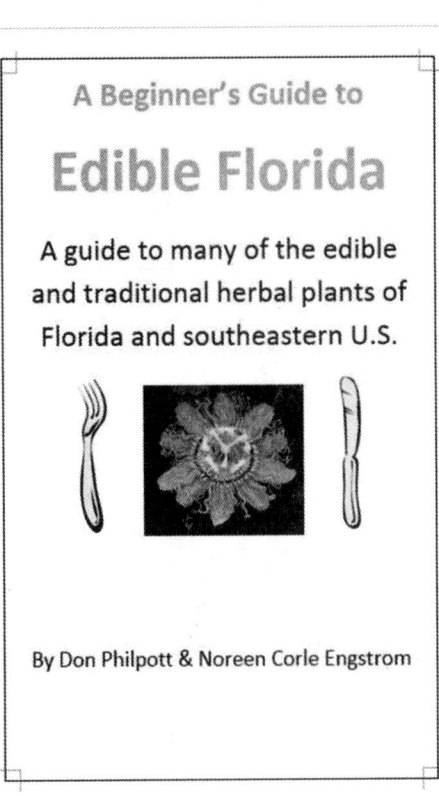

A Beginner's Guide to
Edible Florida

A guide to many of the edible and traditional herbal plants of Florida and southeastern U.S.

By Don Philpott & Noreen Corle Engstrom